ELEMENTARY MATHEMATICS

Grade 5

Manpekin

authorHOUSE®

AuthorHouse™
1663 Liberty Drive
Bloomington, IN 47403
www.authorhouse.com
Phone: 1 (800) 839-8640

Published by AuthorHouse 08/21/2019

ISBN: 978-1-5462-5960-2 (sc)
ISBN: 978-1-5462-5959-6 (e)

Library of Congress Control Number: 2019909080

Print information available on the last page.

Any people depicted in stock imagery provided by Getty Images are models, and such images are being used for illustrative purposes only. Certain stock imagery © Getty Images.

This book is printed on acid-free paper.

CONTENTS

UNIT 1

PROPERTIES OF OPERATIONS

Learning Points

In this unit, we shall

- multiply and divide whole numbers;
- state commutative, associative, and distributive properties;
- state divisibility rules for 2, 3, and 4;
- identify prime and composite numbers;
- find least common multiple (LCM) and greatest common factor (GCF); and
- change from base 10 to bases 2 and 5.

LESSON 1.1

MULTIPLYING AND DIVIDING WHOLE NUMBERS

Numbers like 0, 2, 3, 6, and 7 are whole numbers. We can multiply and divide whole numbers.

When multiplying whole numbers by a one-digit whole number, multiply from right to left. When multiplying by two or more digits, write the individual products and then add.

Sample Work 1

Multiply
$$\begin{array}{r} 63 \\ \times 2 \\ \hline \end{array}$$

Solution

$$\begin{array}{r} 63 \\ \times 2 \\ \hline 126 \end{array}$$ ← multiplicand
← multiplier
← product

Notice that the top number, 63, is called the *multiplicand*. The number by which you multiply, 2, is called the *multiplier*. The answer is called the *product*.

$$\begin{array}{r} \text{multiplicand} \\ \times \text{ multiplier} \\ \hline \text{product} \end{array}$$

We can also multiply horizontally—for example, 63 x 2 = 126.

Multiplicand times multiplier equals product.

Sample Work 2

Multiply 56 x 7.

Solution

$$\begin{array}{r} 4 \\ 56 \\ \underline{\times 7} \\ 392 \end{array}$$

$\longleftarrow$ (7 x 6 = 42. Write the 2 in the ones place. Write the 4 above the tens place.)

(7 x 5 = 35 + 4 = 39)

Sample Work 3

Multiply 28 x 4.

Solution

$$\begin{array}{r} 3 \\ 28 \\ \underline{\times 4} \\ 112 \end{array}$$

$\longleftarrow$ (4 x 8 = 32. Write the 2 in the ones place. Write the 3 above the tens place.)

$\longleftarrow$ (4 x 2 = 8 + 3 = 11)

Sample Work 4

Find the product of 48 x 35.

Solution

$$\begin{array}{r} 48 \\ \underline{\times 35} \\ 240 \\ \underline{144} \\ 1680 \end{array}$$

$\longleftarrow$ (48 x 5 = 240)

$\longleftarrow$ (48 x 3 = 144)

Sample Work 5

Find the product of 819 x 5.

Solution

$$
\begin{array}{r}
819 \\
\times 5 \\
\hline
45 \\
5 \\
40 \\
\hline
4095
\end{array}
$$

45   ⟵ (5 x 9 = 45)
5   ⟵ (5 x 1 = 5)
40   ⟵ (5 x 8 = 40)

Sample Work 6

James donates a collection of books to Galapa Elementary School. He packs eight books in each of four boxes. How many books does James donate?

Solution

4 boxes x 8 books in each box

Total = 4 x 8 = 32

James donates thirty-two books.

Sample Work 7

Divide 45 by 3.

Solution

$$
45 \div 3 = 3\overline{)45}
$$

15 ⟵ quotient
45 ⟵ dividend
3
15
15
0   ⟵ remainder

divisor

Notice that the answer of the division problem is called the *quotient*, the number you are dividing by is called the *divisor*, and the number being divided is called the *dividend*. After that, subtract to get a *remainder*.

When dividing whole numbers, divide in each place-value position from left to right.

$$\text{divisor} \overline{\begin{array}{c} \text{quotient} \\ \text{dividend} \\ \hline \text{remainder} \end{array}}$$

Dividend divided by divisor equals quotient. Quotient times divisor equals dividend.

Sample Work 8

Divide $25 \div 3$.

Solution

$$25 \div 3 \qquad 3 \overline{\begin{array}{r} 8 \\ 25 \\ \underline{24} \\ 1 \end{array}}$$

(8 is the quotient.)

(3 is the divisor; 25 is the dividend.)

(1 is the remainder.)

Sample Work 9

Kofi has seventy-two pieces of carrots. He puts an equal number of carrots into eight bags. How many carrots will be in each bag?

Solution

$$8 \overline{\begin{array}{r} 9 \\ 72 \\ \underline{72} \\ 00 \end{array}}$$

Nine carrots will be in each bag.

Sample Work 10

Daylee has twenty-eight pencils. She separates them equally by placing four in each pencil case. How many pencil cases does Daylee have?

Solution

4 pencils in each group

28 total pencils

$28 \div 4 = 7$

Daylee has seven pencil cases.

Practice

Multiply.

1. 53	2. 31	3. 84	4. 85	5. 12	6. 19	7. 23	8. 65	9. 58	10. 22
x2	x5	x4	x2	x6	x5	x8	x4	x3	x33

11. 81	12. 92	13. 58	14. 48
x2	x2	x3	x11

15. Juana buys four bags of candy. There are twenty-seven pieces of candy in each bag. How many pieces of candy does Juana buy?

16. Mr. Marcus will harvest beans for five days. He is expected to harvest seventy-six bags of beans each day. How many bags of beans will Mr. Marcus harvest from the farm?

17. Mariana prepares fifteen plates of sandwich for her children's party. There are nine pieces of shrimp on each plate. How many pieces of shrimp does Mariana prepare?

18. Morlue bought 6 bags of corn. There were 210 pieces of corn in each bag. How many pieces of corn did Morlue buy?

19. Quiah's sister gives him 5 packages of stickers. There are 840 stickers in each package. How many stickers does Quiah's sister give him in all?

Find the product.

20. 4203	21. 678	22. 769	23. 126	24. 237
x2	x9	x8	x7	x35

Multiply and name the parts.

25. 41 x 2   26. 63 x 6   27. 18 x 12   28. 93 x 4   29. 55 x 8   30. 17 x 27   31. 69 x 11

32. 35 x 13   33. 14 x 12   34. 64 x 14   35. 73 x 12   36. 81 x 21   37. 94 x 21

Divide.

1. 51 ÷ 5   2. 87 ÷ 4   3. 431 ÷ 3   4. 441 ÷ 21   5. 54 ÷ 2   6. 980 ÷ 35

7. 343 ÷ 7   8. 729 ÷ 9   9. 512 ÷ 8   10. 625 ÷ 5   11. 96 ÷ 2   12. 93 ÷ 7

13. A construction company has seventy-five dollars to buy paint. If each can of paint costs five dollars, how many cans of paint can the company buy?

Find the quotient.

14. $4\overline{)232}$ 15. $5\overline{)783}$ 16. $2\overline{)128}$ 17. $3\overline{)729}$ 18. $6\overline{)216}$ 19. $4\overline{)256}$

20. $572 \div 4$ 21. $411 \div 3$ 22. $417 \div 3$ 23. $128 \div 2$ 24. $729 \div 3$ 25 $216 \div 6$

26. $256 \div 4$

Divide using the division box and name the parts.

27. $95 \div 3$ 28. $860 \div 10$ 29. $310 \div 100$ 30. $575 \div 23$ 31. $86 \div 2$ 32. $196 \div 7$

33. $846 \div 3$

LESSON 1.2

WRITING AND STATING COMMUTATIVE PROPERTIES

When we add two numbers—for example, 2 + 3—the order in which they are written or added does not change the sum. This is called *commutative property of addition*. Also when we multiply two numbers—for example, 2 x 3—the order in which they are written or multiplied does not change the product. This is called the *commutative property of multiplication*.

Sample Work 1

3 + 4 = 4 + 3 ⟵ horizontal form

7 = 7

Sample Work 2

$$
\begin{array}{ll}
5 & 8 \\
\underline{+8} & \underline{+5} \\
13 & 13
\end{array}
$$
⟵ vertical form

Sample Work 3

Write the missing number.

7 + 6 = 6 + ☐

Solution

7 + 6 = 6 + ☐

7 + 6 = 6 + 7

The missing number is 7.

Sample Work 4

Write the missing number.

$500 + \boxed{} = 843 + 500$

Solution

$500 + \boxed{} = 843 + 500$

$500 + \boxed{843} = 843 + 500$

The missing number is 843.

Sample Work 5

$3 \times 2 = 2 \times 3$

$6 = 6$

Sample Work 6

$5 \times 7 = 7 \times 5$

Sample Work 7

Write the missing number.

$4 \times 221 = 221 \times \boxed{}$

Solution

$4 \times 221 = 221 \times \boxed{}$

$4 \times 221 = 221 \times \boxed{4}$

The missing number is 4.

Practice

1. State the commutative property of addition.

2. State the commutative property of multiplication.

3. Write three examples of the commutative property of addition.

4. Write three examples of the commutative property of multiplication.

Write the missing number.

5. $\boxed{} + 6 = 6 + 3$

6. $5 + 1 = 1 + \boxed{}$

7. $1 + 2 = \boxed{} + 1$

8. $8 + \boxed{} = 5 + 8$

9. $7 + \boxed{} = 3 + 7$

10. $4 + 4 = 4 + \boxed{}$

11. $10 + 30 = 30 + \boxed{}$

12. $\boxed{} + 14 = 14 + 23$

13. $\boxed{} + 10 = 10 + 453$

14. $453 + \boxed{} = 7 + 453$

15. $6 \times 3 = 3 \times \boxed{}$

16. $1 \times 5 = 5 \times \boxed{}$

17. $2 \times 1 = 1 \times \boxed{}$

18. $5 \times \boxed{} = 8 \times 5$

19. $3 \times \boxed{} = 7 \times 3$

20. $30 \times \boxed{} = 10 \times 30$

21. $\boxed{} \times 23 = 23 \times 14$

22. $\boxed{} \times 61 = 61 \times 10$

23. $\boxed{} \times 45 = 45 \times 7$

24. $\boxed{} \times 4 = 4 \times 4$

LESSON 1.3

WRITING AND STATING ASSOCIATIVE PROPERTIES

When we add or multiply three numbers, the order in which we group them does not change the sum or product. This is called *associative property*.

Sample Work 1

$(3 + 2) + 4 = 3 + (2 + 4)$

$5 + 4 = 3 + 6$

$9 = 9$

Sample Work 2

$(5 \text{ boys} + 3 \text{ boys}) + 4 \text{ boys} = 5 \text{ boys} + (3 \text{ boys} + 4 \text{ boys})$

$8 \text{ boys} + 4 \text{ boys} = 5 \text{ boys} + 7 \text{ boys}$

$12 \text{ boys} = 12 \text{ boys}$

Sample Work 3

$(596 + 31) + 4 = 596 + (31 + 4)$

Sample Work 4

Find the missing number.

$(37 + 19) + 5 = \boxed{} + (19 + 5)$

The missing number is 37.

Sample Work 5

$(4 \times 3) \times 2 = 4 \times (3 \times 2)$

$\qquad 12 \times 2 = 4 \times 6$

$\qquad\qquad 24 = 24$

Sample Work 6

$(6 \times 5) \times 3 = 6 \times (5 \times 3)$

$\qquad 30 \times 3 = 6 \times 15$

$\qquad\qquad 90 = 90$

Sample Work 7

Find the missing number.

$12 \times (\boxed{} \times 4) = (12 \times 8) \times 4$

The missing number is 8.

Practice

1. State the associative property of addition.

2. State the associative property of multiplication.

3. Write two examples of the associative property of multiplication.

4. Write two examples of the associative property of addition.

Write the missing number.

5. $(6 + 3) + 1 = 6 + (3 + \boxed{})$ 6. $(1 + 5) + 2 = 1 + (5 + \boxed{})$ 7. $(8 + 2) + \boxed{} = 8 + (2 + 5)$

8. $(7 + 3) + \boxed{} = 7 + (3 + 4)$ 9. $(4 + \boxed{}) + 6 = 4 + (9 + 6)$ 10. $\frac{2}{7} + (\boxed{} + 1) = (\frac{2}{7} + 5) + 1$

11. $341 + (\boxed{} + 10) = (341 + 6) + 10$ 12. $7 + (\boxed{} + 9) = (7 + 543) + 9$

13. $8 + (\boxed{} + 6) = (8 + 64) + 6$

14. $5 + (\boxed{} + 3) = (5 + 78) + 3$

15. $\boxed{} \times (3 \times 6) = (1 \times 3) \times 6$

16. $\boxed{} \times (5 \times 1) = (2 \times 5) \times 1$

17. $\boxed{} \times (2 \times 8) = (5 \times 2) \times 8$

18. $\boxed{} \times (7 \times 4) = (3 \times 7) \times 4$

19. $\boxed{} \times (9 \times 6) = (4 \times 9) \times 6$

20. $(\frac{2}{7} \times 5) \times 1 = \boxed{} \times (5 \times 1)$

21. $(10 \times 6) \times 341 = \boxed{} \times (6 \times 341)$

22. $(7 \times 543) \times 9 = \boxed{} \times (543 \times 9)$

23. $(8 \times 64) \times 6 = \boxed{} \times (64 \times 6)$

24. $(5 \times 78) \times 3 = \boxed{} \times (78 \times 3)$

LESSON 1.4

WRITING AND STATING DISTRIBUTIVE PROPERTIES

We can also use distributive property to multiply.

Sample Work 1

Expand 2 (3 + 4).

Solution

2 (3 + 4) = (2 x 3) + (2 x 4) ---- (Multiply each number in the parenthesis by 2.)

Sample Work 2

Expand 3 (4 + 1).

Solution

3(4 + 1) = (3 x 4) + (3 x 1) ---- (Multiply each number in the parenthesis by 3.)

Sample Work 3

Expand 5(6 - 4).

Solution

5(6 - 4) = (5 x 6) - (5 x 4)

Notice that the number outside the parenthesis is multiplied by each number inside the parenthesis.

Practice

Expand.

1. $6(6 + 7)$ 2. $3(5 + 1)$ 3. $5(8 + 10)$ 4. $10(2 + 1)$

5. $9(20 + 30)$ 6. $7(4 + 2)$ 7. $3(1 + 1)$ 8. $26(1 + 2)$

9. $3(7 + 8)$ 10. $3(50 + 600)$ 11. $6(7 - 6)$ 12. $3(5 - 1)$

13. $5(10 - 8)$ 14. $10(2 - 1)$ 15. $8(23 - 7)$ 16. $23(8 - 1)$

17. $5(600 - 8)$ 18. $9(30 - 20)$ 19. $2(2 - 1)$ 20. $3(1 - 1)$

21. Write five examples of distributive property of addition.

22. Write five examples of distributive property of subtraction.

LESSON 1.5

DIVISIBILITY RULES FOR 2, 3, AND 4

A number is divisible by another number if the remainder is zero. For example, 34 is divisible by 2. When we divide 34 by 2, the reminder is 0.

```
        17
   2 | 34
        2
       14
       14
        0  ——— (Remainder is zero.)
```

A number is divisible by 3 if the sum of the digits is divisible by 3.

Sample Work 1

Is 45 divisible by 3?

Solution

Find out if the sum of 4 + 5, which is 9, is divisible by 3.

4 + 5 = 9

9 is divisible by 3, so 45 is divisible by 3.

Sample Work 2

Is 52 divisible by 3?

Solution

52 = 5 + 2 = 7

7 is not divisible by 3, so 52 is not divisible by 3.

Sample Work 3

Is 212 divisible by 4?

Solution

2<u>12</u> ÷ 4

A number is divisible by 4 if the last two digits are divisible by 4. The last two digits of 212 is 12. Divide the last two digits, 12, by 4.

$$
\begin{array}{r}
3 \\
4\overline{)12} \\
12 \\
\hline
0
\end{array}
$$

Yes, 212 is divisible by 4 since the last two digits, which is 12, is divisible by 4.

A number is divisible by 2 if the last digit is an even number or any whole number ending in 0.

Sample Work 4

Is 18 divisible by 2?

Solution

Yes, 18 is divisible by 2 since the last digit, which is 8, is divisible by 2.

Practice

Tell or write which number is divisible by 2.

1. 29	2. 134	3. 55	4. 88	5. 912	6. 754
7. 15	8. 18	9. 24	10. 38	11. 100	12. 828
13. 16	14. 58	15. 16	16. 550	17. 968	18. 335

19. 574   20. 691

Write which number is divisible by 3.

1.	318	2.	345	3.	414	4.	201	5.	156	6.	5,670	7.	239
8.	617	9.	725	10.	315	11.	5,931	12.	876	13.	786	14.	509
15.	425	16.	147	17.	823	18.	346	19.	572	20.	3,471		

Tell which number is divisible by 4.

1.	9,032	2.	132	3.	516	4.	988	5.	675	6.	395	7.	105
8.	1,825	9.	780	10.	890	11.	88	12.	1,380	13.	124	14.	592
15.	156												

LESSON 1.6

IDENTIFYING PRIME AND COMPOSITE NUMBERS

Prime Numbers

A natural number divisible by exactly two natural numbers is a prime number—for example, 2, 3, 7...

Is 1 a prime number?

One is divisible by 1, and 1 is divisible by only itself. One is divisible by only one number, so 1 is not prime number.

Is 2 a prime number because it is divisible by 1 and itself?

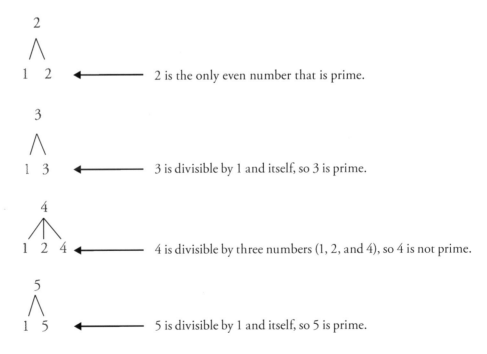

A prime number is a number that can be divided by only 1 and itself. For example, 7 is a prime number since no other number besides 1 and 7 divides into it without a remainder.

Some prime numbers are 2, 3, 5, 7, 11, 13, 17, 19, 23, 29, 31, 37, 41, 43, 47, 53, 59, 61, 67, 71, 73, 79, 83, 89, and 97. Notice that this is a list of prime numbers up to 100.

Composite Numbers

Numbers like 4, 6, 9, 15, 21, and 22 are composite numbers. A composite number is a number that has at least one factor other than 1 and itself.

Some composite numbers are 4, 6, 8, 9, 10, 12, 14, 15, 16, 18, 20, 21, 22, 24, 25, 26, 27, 28, 30, 32, 33, 34, 35, 36, 38, 39, 40, 42, 44, 45, 46, 48, 49, and 50.

Sample Work 1

Tell if prime or composite number: 33, 43, 49, and 28.

Solution

a.   33 is a composite number since it has two other factors (11 and 3) besides 1 and itself.

b.   43 is a prime number since it has only 1 and itself as factors.

c.   49 is a prime number since it has only 1 and itself as factors.

d.   28 is a composite number since it has at least two other factors (2, 4, and 14) besides 1 and itself.

Practice

1. List all prime numbers less than 150.

2. List all prime numbers from 100 to 240.

3. Make a table of all prime numbers from 200 to 300.

4. List all composite numbers less than 50.

5. Is 1 a prime number? If no, why?

6. Is 1 a composite number? If yes, why?

7. Show as prime or composite: 91, 92, 93, 94, 95, 96, 97, 98, 99, 100, 101, 103, 113, 114, and 115.

8. List all composite numbers from 50 to 80.

5. List all prime numbers from 50 to 80.

LESSON 1.7

LCM AND GCF OF THREE NUMBERS

LCM is least common multiple, and GCF is greatest common factor. The LCM of numbers is the smallest number, not zero, that is a multiple of the numbers. The greatest factor that divides two numbers is the GCF. To find the GCF, list the prime factors of each number.

Sample Work 1

Find the LCM of 2, 3, and 4.

Solution

Multiples of 2: 2, 4, 6, 8, 10, 12, 14, 16, 18, 20, 22, 24 …

Multiples of 3: 3, 6, 9, 12, 15, 18, 21, 24 …

Multiples of 4: 4, 8, 12, 16, 20, 24 …

Common multiples of 2, 3, and 4 are 12 and 24.

Smallest common multiple of 2, 3, and 4 is 12.

So, 12 is the LCM of 2, 3, and 4.

Sample Work 2

Find the GCF of 8, 4, and 6.

Solution

List the factors of each number.

Factors of 8: 1, 2, 4, 8

Factors of 4: 1, 2, 4

Factors of 6: 1, 2, 3, 6

Common factor for 8, 4, and 6 is 2.

So, 2 is the GCF for 8, 4 and 6.

Practice

Find the LCM of the numbers.

1.	4, 6, 2	2.	3, 4, 8	3.	5, 3, 15	4.	15, 30, 5	5.	40, 10, 50
6.	36, 12, 6	7.	18, 12, 24	8.	9, 3, 12	9.	4, 6, 3	10.	8, 4, 2
11.	3, 2, 5	12.	3, 5, 12	13.	25, 50, 15	14.	21, 35, 49	15.	20, 10, 30

Find the GCF for the numbers.

1.	3, 5, 15	2.	2, 5, 6	3.	6, 10, 15	4.	3, 5, 6	5.	2, 3, 6
6.	2, 4, 10	7.	30, 40, 50	8.	20, 30, 40	9.	9, 3, 15	10.	27, 21, 9
11.	32, 8, 4	12.	30, 12, 6	13.	2, 3, 4	14.	3, 5, 4	15.	10, 15, 30
16.	5, 10, 15	17.	9, 3, 8	18.	7, 21, 3	19.	4, 8, 32	20.	3, 18, 24

LESSON 1.8

CHANGING BASE 10 TO BASES 2 AND 5

We can change from one base to another.

Decimal (base 10) $\longrightarrow$ 0, 1, 2, 3, 4, 5, 6, 7, 8, 9 Binary (base 2) $\longrightarrow$ 0, 1

Sample Work 1

Change 33_{10} to bases 2 and 5

Solution

$33_{10} = \text{—}$base 2 $33_{10} = \text{—}$base 5

2	33	1
2	16	0
2	8	0
2	4	0
2	2	0
	1	

5	33	3
5	6	1
	1	

$33_{10} = 113_5$

$33_{10} = 100001_2$

Sample Work 2

Change 70_{10} to bases 2 and 5.

Solution

$70_{10} =$ —base 2 $\qquad\qquad$ $70_{10} =$ —base 5

2	70	0
2	35	1
2	17	1
2	8	0
2	4	0
2	2	0
	1	

5	70	0
5	14	4
	2	

$70_{10} = 240_5$

$70_{10} = 1000110_2$

Practice

Change the following base 10 numerals to base 2.

1. 85_{10} 2. 93_{10} 3. 67_{10} 4. 39_{10} 5. 88_{10} 6. 92_{10} 7. 64_{10} 8. 45_{10} 9. 99_{10}

10. 96_{10} 11. 86_{10} 12. 75_{10} 13. 68_{10} 14. 55_{10} 15. 22_{10} 16. 25_{10} 17. 36_{10}

18. 62_{10} 19. 28_{10} 20. 44_{10} 21. 53_{10} 22. 43_{10} 23. 56_{10} 24. 38_{10} 25. 72_{10}

MANPEKIN

Change the following base 10 numerals to base 5.

1. 42_{10} 2. 34_{10} 3. 27_{10} 4. 33_{10} 5. 59_{10} 6. 87_{10}

7. 55_{10} 8. 57_{10} 9. 80_{10} 10. 39_{10} 11. 43_{10} 12. 93_{10}

13. 75_{10} 14. 94_{10} 15. 51_{10} 16. 48_{10} 17. 91_{10} 18. 21_{10}

19. 58_{10} 20. 73_{10}

UNIT 2
DECIMAL AND NUMBER THEORY

Learning Points

In this unit, we shall

- add and subtract decimals; and
- multiply and divide decimals.

LESSON 2.1

ADDING AND SUBTRACTING DECIMALS

When adding decimal numbers, write or place the decimal points directly under each other. Make the numbers equal by adding zeros so the numbers have the same number of decimal places. Then add using the same rule for adding whole numbers.

Sample Work 1

Add 7.84 + 6.75.

Solution

$$
\begin{array}{r}
7.84 \quad \longleftarrow \quad \text{Addend} \\
+\ \underline{6.75} \quad \longleftarrow \quad \text{Addend} \\
14.59 \quad \longleftarrow \quad \text{Sum}
\end{array}
$$

Sample Work 2

Add 2.453 + 1.2.

Solution

$$
\begin{array}{r}
2.453 \\
+\ \underline{1.2} \\
\end{array}
$$

$$
\begin{array}{r}
2.453 \\
+\ \underline{1.\mathbf{200}} \quad \text{(Add two zeros to make the numbers equal, and then add.)} \\
3.653
\end{array}
$$

Sample Work 3

Add 3.04 + .652.

Solution

$$3.04\mathbf{0}$$
$$+ \underline{\mathbf{0}.652}$$
$$3.692$$

Sample Work 4

During the farming season last year, Jolo estimated that his corn crop needed 390.1 gallons of water. He also estimated that his banana crop needed 143.2 gallons of water. How many gallons of water did Jolo plan to use in all?

Solution

Corn crop: 390.1 gallons of water

Banana crop: 143.2 gallons of water

390.1 gal + 143.2 gal = 533.3 gallons

Jolo planned to use 533.3 gallons of water

Sample Work 5

Mamiata is in a 100 meters swimming race. She swims the first half of the race in 3.4 minutes and the last half of the race in 3.3 minutes. How long will it take her to swim the whole race?

Solution

First half of the race: 3.4 minutes

Last half of the race: 3.3 minutes

3.4 min + 3.3 min = 6.7 min

It will take 6.7 minutes to swim the whole race.

When subtracting decimal numbers, write or place the decimal points directly under each other. Make the numbers equal by adding zeros so that both numbers have the same number of decimal places. Then subtract using the same rule for subtracting whole numbers.

Sample Work 6

Subtract 6.467 − 1.25.

Solution

$$
\begin{array}{r}
6.467 \\
-\ \underline{1.25} \\
\end{array}
$$

$$
\begin{array}{r}
6.467 \\
-\ \underline{1.25\mathbf{0}} \\
5.217 \\
\end{array}
$$
(Add one zero to make the numbers equal and then subtract.)

Sample Work 7

Subtract 5.685 − 2.34.

Solution

$$
\begin{array}{r}
5.685 \\
-\ \underline{2.340} \\
3.345 \\
\end{array}
$$
← minuend
← subtrahend
← difference

Sample Work 8

Subtract 23.78 − 4.6.

Solution

$$
\begin{array}{r}
23.78 \\
-\ \underline{4.6\ \ } \\
19.18 \\
\end{array}
$$

$$
\begin{array}{r}
23.78 \\
-\ \underline{04.60} \\
19.18 \\
\end{array}
$$
(Add two zeros to make the numbers equal and then subtract.)

Sample Work 9

A Lone Star phone company has a total of 952.0 customers living in Asia and Africa. Of those customers, 643.0 live in Africa. How many of the customers live in Asia?

Solution

Total customers living in Asia and Africa: 952.0

Customers living in Africa: 643.0

Customers in Asia = Total customers (952.0) - Customers in Africa (643.0)

Customers in Asia = 952.0 – 643.0

Customers in Asia = 309.0

There are 309.0 customers in Asia.

Sample Work 10

Recently Zwedru Elementary School tuition was reduced by $110.60. If the tuition were $510.25 before, how much is the tuition now?

Solution

Tuition before: $510.25

Tuition reduced by: $110.60

Tuition now = Tuition before (510.25) - Tuition reduced ($110.60)

Tuition now = $510.25 - $110.60

Tuition now = $399.65

The tuition now is $399.65.

Practice

Add.

1.	2.42	2.	3.456	3.	6.15	4.	0.168	5.	8.001	6.	3.1
	+1.3		+7.1		+6.05		+5.2		+2.5		+1.1091
7.	0.46	8.	2.09	9.	3.58	10.	0.87	11.	$7.81	12.	$0.75
	+0.43		+5.45		+2.14		+0.16		+$9.56		+$2.32

13. $\begin{array}{r} 2.846 \\ +3.250 \\ \hline \end{array}$ 14. $7.468 + 0.981$ 15. $\begin{array}{r} 73.6 \\ +9.8 \\ \hline \end{array}$ 16. $63.53 + 91.4$ 17. $8.589 + 5.96$

18. $8.075 + 14.31$ 19. $9.807 + 15.23$ 20. $0.823 + 6.54$ 21. $604.7 + 5.68$

22. $7.006 + 60.57$ 23. $52.106 + 3.012$

24. Doma spent $525 to buy his child's school uniform. He was left with $31.75 after buying the uniform. How much money did Doma have before?

25. While traveling to Cape Palmas last week, Korto drove 54.2 miles on the first day, 48.1 miles on the second day, 25 miles on the third day, and 17.4 miles on the fourth day. How many miles did Korto drive in all in the four days?

26. Yempu purchased twenty dozen school bags for $300.20, five dozen books for $150.43, and three dozen pens for $31. How much money did Yempu spend?

27. In 2017, the weather forecaster at the school recorded 86.4 millimeters of rainfall in October, 115.7 millimeters in November, and 100.54 millimeters in December. How many millimeters of total rainfall were recorded during these three months?

28. Matthew walked 2.1 kilometers on Monday, 2.3 kilometers on Tuesday, 1.58 kilometers on Wednesday, and 1.95 kilometers on Thursday. What is the total distance he walked in the four days?

Subtract

1. $\begin{array}{r} \$3.86 \\ -\$2.76 \\ \hline \end{array}$ 2. $\begin{array}{r} 7.821 \\ -5.4 \\ \hline \end{array}$ 3. $\begin{array}{r} 10.006 \\ -8.007 \\ \hline \end{array}$ 4. $\begin{array}{r} \$92.01 \\ -\$86.13 \\ \hline \end{array}$ 5. $\begin{array}{r} 32 \\ -25.007 \\ \hline \end{array}$ 6. $\begin{array}{r} 2.155 \\ -1.046 \\ \hline \end{array}$

7. $\begin{array}{r} 1.809 \\ -1.804 \\ \hline \end{array}$ 8. $\begin{array}{r} \$74.46 \\ -\$42.15 \\ \hline \end{array}$ 9. $\begin{array}{r} 85.3 \\ -23.67 \\ \hline \end{array}$ 10. $\begin{array}{r} 7.67 \\ -4.84 \\ \hline \end{array}$ 11. $\begin{array}{r} 60.18 \\ -40.09 \\ \hline \end{array}$ 12. $\begin{array}{r} 4.8 \\ -2.6 \\ \hline \end{array}$

13. $\begin{array}{r} 304.46 \\ -96.56 \\ \hline \end{array}$ 14. $4.85 - 1.596$ 15. $18.05 - 4.3$ 16. $\$537.43 - \$89.76$

17. $424.506 - 383.939$ 18. $\$28.93 - \$13$ 19. $4.9 - 2.3$ 20. $54.12 - 7.13$

21. $81.48 - 3.98$ 22. $\$329.83 - \$251.32$ 23. $98.4 - 54.67$

24. Koffi needs $25.30 to buy his school materials. He has $15.50. How much additional amount of money does he need?

25. Jusu purchased three bags of apple for $150.25. He paid with a $200 bill. How much change did Jusu receive?

26. On July 26, John walks 3.9 miles to a party, and Nina walks 5.6 miles to the party. How much farther does Nina walk than John?

27. Papa had $500.75 to buy his children's uniforms. After buying the uniforms, he was left with $85.96. How much did Papa spend?

28. Anna bought 11.4 kilograms of sugar and used 7.8 kilograms of the sugar to make cake. How much sugar was not used?

29. Sumo buys his new science books costing $15.50. He gives $20 to the bookseller. How much change will Sumo receive back?

30. Koluba went to a grocery store and purchased 25.3 pounds of beans and corn. Of the 25.3 pounds, 11.9 pounds was corn. How many pounds were beans?

31. Weata earns $210.10. She buys two bags of flour for $108.50. How much money will be left with Weata?

32. Mrs. Keita earns $500. She gives $205 to Tar to buy books. How much money does she have left with her?

33. Omotoye had $625.50. He gave Okonokhua $67.85 to buy his shoes for the upcoming children's party. How much money did Omotoye have left with him?

34. James plans to withdraw $75.50 from his bank account tomorrow to enable him to get his school materials. Now he has $250 in his account. How much money will be left in James' account after the withdrawal?

35. Tokpa and Sano traveled 95.6 miles and 130.3 miles, respectively. Who traveled more distance than the other and by how many miles?

36. Cooper bought a chocolate pack from Walmart for $92. He paid $95.15 at the checkout. How much money did he receive back in change at the checkout?

37. Sunyma, Sadyma, and Mondyma are sisters. Sunyma is 3.5 feet tall, Sadyma is 4.2 feet tall, and Mondyma is 5.7 feet tall. How much taller is Mondyma than Sunyma?

38. Before the housing project, there were 200.0 houses in Zao Township. Now there are 350.0 houses in all in Zao Township. How many new houses were built during the housing project?

39. Tarley scored 372.1 points while playing a video game. She and her nephew together have a total of 605.6 points. How many points does Tarley's nephew have?

LESSON 2.2

MULTIPLYING AND DIVIDING DECIMALS

When multiplying decimal numbers, the number of decimal places in the product is the sum of the decimal places in the multiplicand and multiplier.

Sample Work 1

Multiply   7.1
                x5.4

Solution

$$
\begin{array}{r}
7.1 \\
x5.4 \\
\hline
284 \\
355 \\
\hline
38.34
\end{array}
$$

7.1 ⟵ one decimal place in the multiplicand

x5.4 ⟵ one decimal place in the multiplier

355 ⟵ partial products

38.34 ⟵ two decimal places in the product

Sample Work 2

Multiply 3.2 x .6.

Solution

3.2 ⟵ one decimal place

x.6 ⟵ one decimal place ⟩ two decimal places

1.92 ⟵ two decimal places in the product

Sample Work 3

Multiply 5.4 x 0.13.

Solution

$$5.4 \longleftarrow \text{one decimal place}$$
$$\underline{\times 0.13} \longleftarrow \text{two decimal places} \quad \Big\rangle \quad \text{three decimal places}$$
$$162$$
$$\underline{54}$$
$$0.702 \longleftarrow \text{three decimal places in the product}$$

Sample Work 4

One big pack of crayons weighs 43.2 grams. How much do twenty packs weigh?

Solution

43.2 grams x 20 packs = 864 grams

Twenty packs will weigh 864 grams.

Division of decimals is similar to division of whole numbers. When there is a decimal in the divisor, make the divisor a whole number by moving the decimal to the right to make the divisor into a whole number.

Sample Work 5

Divide 4.032 ÷ 4.

Solution

$$
\begin{array}{r}
1.008 \\
4\overline{)4.032} \\
\underline{4} \\
0 \\
\underline{0} \\
3 \\
\underline{0} \\
32 \\
\underline{32} \\
0
\end{array}
$$

Sample Work 6

Divide .8614 ÷ .12.

Solution

$$.12\overline{)\,.8614}$$

Move the decimals in both the divisor and dividend two places to the right to make the divisor into a whole number and then divide.

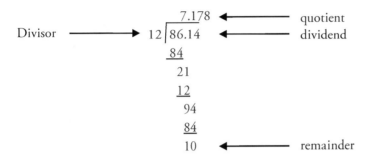

Sample Work 7

Divide 36 ÷ .3.

Solution

```
   120
 3)360
   3
   6
   6
   0
   0
```

.3)360. Move the decimal one place to the right and add a zero to the dividend.

Practice

Multiply.

1.	84.4	2.	48.5	3.	0.2	4.	0.4	5.	4.34	6.	.121	7.	0.112
	x14.5		x15.4		x0.5		x0.8		x1.8		x0.2		x0.02

8.	7.25	9.	1.2	10.	4.5	11.	$3.06	12.	0.64	13.	7.9	14.	$41.50
	x0.01		x9.8		x5.3		x$0.6		x6.81		x0.01		x$0.8

15. 61.8   16. 12.22 x 3.2   17. 2.02 x 1.1   18. .68 x 1.4   19. 4.14 x 100
     x.008
              20. 10 x 2.07   21. 6 x .3   22. 5 x 1.2   23. 1.03 x 2.3

24. .003 x .2   25. .025 x 8   26. 1.03 x 2.3   27. 9 x .2   28. 2.1 x .5   29. 6 x .5

30. 7.4 x .6   31. 202 x 2.1   32. .65 x .7

Divide.

1.   614.25 ÷ 31.5   2.   77.0 ÷ .36   3.   770.4 ÷ 3.6   4.   185.44 ÷ 6.1   5.   29.6 ÷ 0.08

6.   1.92 ÷ 0.6   7.   19.2 ÷ 3.2   8.   0.006 ÷ 0.2   9.   1.8 ÷ 0.3   10. 18. 32 ÷ 0.8

11. 1.832 ÷ 0.04   12. 183.2 ÷ 0.4   13. 183.2 ÷ 0.08 14. 40 ÷ 12.8   15. 1.634 ÷ 0.43

16. 18.75 ÷ 5.39   17. .63 ÷ 7   18. .0016 ÷ .8   19. 72 ÷ .4   20. 35.6 ÷ .4

21. 12 ÷ .03   22. 972 ÷ .180   23. 670.8 ÷ .78

UNIT 3
FRACTIONS

Learning Points

In this unit, we shall

- find equivalent fractions;
- compare and order fractions;
- add and subtract fractions; and
- multiply and divide fractions.

LESSON 3.1

FINDING EQUIVALENT FRACTIONS

To get the equivalent fraction, multiply both the numerator and denominator of the fraction by the same number.

Sample Work 1

Find the equivalent of $\frac{3}{4}$.

Solution

$$\frac{3}{4} = \frac{3 \times 2}{4 \times 2} \longleftarrow \text{multiplying both numerator and denominator by 2}$$

$$= \frac{6}{8}$$

The equivalent is $\frac{6}{8}$.

Sample Work 2

Write the equivalent of $\frac{7}{8}$.

Solution

$$\frac{7}{8} \times \frac{4}{4} = \frac{7 \times 4}{8 \times 4} = \frac{28}{32}$$

The equivalent is $\frac{28}{32}$

Sample Work 3

Find the equivalent of $\frac{5}{7}$.

Solution

$\frac{5}{7} = \frac{5}{7} \times \frac{3}{3}$ ⟵ Multiplying both numerator and denominator by 3.

$= \frac{15}{21}$

The equivalent is $\frac{15}{21}$.

Practice

Find the equivalent.

1. $\frac{7}{3}$ 2. $\frac{12}{9}$ 3. $\frac{4}{5}$ 4. $\frac{6}{5}$ 5. $\frac{1}{10}$ 6. $\frac{12}{20}$

7. $\frac{9}{21}$ 8. $\frac{1}{6}$ 9. $\frac{2}{24}$ 10. $\frac{5}{6}$ 11. $\frac{1}{3}$ 12. $\frac{2}{5}$ 13. $\frac{3}{7}$

14. $\frac{5}{10}$ 15. $\frac{3}{11}$ 16. $\frac{1}{2}$ 17. $\frac{1}{5}$ 18. $\frac{2}{6}$ 19. $\frac{3}{14}$ 20. $\frac{2}{7}$ 21. $\frac{7}{9}$ 22. $\frac{5}{8}$

23. $\frac{5}{9}$ 24. $\frac{6}{13}$ 25. $\frac{2}{17}$ 26. $\frac{1}{9}$

LESSON 3.2

COMPARING AND ORDERING FRACTIONS

We can use < ("is less than"), > ("is greater than"), or = ("is equal to") to compare two fractions.

Sample Work 1

Compare the following fractions.

a. $\dfrac{2}{3} \square \dfrac{1}{3}$ b. $\dfrac{5}{9} \square \dfrac{7}{9}$

Solution a. $\dfrac{2}{3} \square \dfrac{1}{3}$

Notice that the fractions have the same denominator, 3. Look at the two numerators.

Which one is greater than the other? The number 2 is greater than 1.

So $\dfrac{2}{3} > \dfrac{1}{3}$. We can write $\dfrac{2}{3} \boxed{>} \dfrac{1}{3}$.

Solution b. $\dfrac{5}{9} \square \dfrac{7}{9}$

Notice again that the two fractions have the same denominator. Look at the two numerators.

Which one is greater than the other? The number 7 is greater than 5.

So $\dfrac{5}{9} < \dfrac{7}{9}$. We can write $\dfrac{5}{9} \boxed{<} \dfrac{7}{9}$.

To compare and order fractions, rewrite all the fractions with a common denominator. Then order the fractions by ordering the numerators. You may rewrite the fractions as decimals and then order them.

Sample Work 2

Order $\frac{1}{3}$, $\frac{3}{4}$, and $\frac{2}{3}$ from least to greatest.

Solution

$\frac{1}{3}$, $\frac{3}{4}$, and $\frac{2}{3}$

Rewrite the fractions with common denominator or write as decimals.

$$\frac{1}{3} \times \frac{4}{4} = \frac{4}{12} = 0.33 \qquad \frac{3}{4} \times \frac{3}{3} = \frac{9}{12} = 0.75 \qquad \frac{2}{3} \times \frac{4}{4} = \frac{8}{12} = 0.67$$

We now have $\frac{4}{12}$ or 0.33, $\frac{9}{12}$ or 0.75, and $\frac{8}{12}$ or 0.67.

Order these new numerators: 4 < 8 < 9. We may also order the decimals: 0.33 < 0.67 < 0.75.

So $\frac{1}{3}$, $\frac{2}{3}$, and $\frac{3}{4}$ are in order from least to greatest

When two fractions have different denominators but the same numerator, the fraction with the larger denominator is smaller.

Sample Work 3

Is $\frac{3}{7}$ greater than $\frac{3}{8}$?

Solution

Yes, $\frac{3}{7} > \frac{3}{8}$ because $\frac{3}{8}$ has a larger denominator.

Practice

Tell which fraction is greater than the other. Use >, <, or =.

1. $\frac{3}{4}$ ☐ $\frac{1}{8}$ 2. $\frac{4}{7}$ ☐ $\frac{5}{11}$ 3. $\frac{6}{9}$ ☐ $\frac{3}{10}$ 4. $\frac{1}{8}$ ☐ $\frac{2}{5}$ 5. $\frac{3}{5}$ ☐ $\frac{3}{5}$

6. $\frac{2}{3}$ ☐ $\frac{1}{5}$ 7. $\frac{1}{2}$ ☐ $\frac{1}{4}$ 8. $\frac{3}{4}$ ☐ $\frac{1}{7}$ 9. $\frac{5}{8}$ ☐ $\frac{3}{8}$ 10. $\frac{1}{6}$ ☐ $\frac{1}{7}$

Compare the fractions. Use <, >, or =

1. $\dfrac{0}{9}$ ☐ $\dfrac{1}{9}$ 2. $\dfrac{4}{7}$ ☐ $\dfrac{5}{11}$ 3. $\dfrac{2}{3}$ ☐ $\dfrac{1}{3}$ 4. $\dfrac{3}{5}$ ☐ $\dfrac{3}{5}$

5. $\dfrac{7}{12}$ ☐ $\dfrac{2}{12}$ 6. $\dfrac{3}{30}$ ☐ $\dfrac{9}{30}$ 7. $\dfrac{4}{7}$ ☐ $\dfrac{5}{7}$ 8. $\dfrac{7}{4}$ ☐ $\dfrac{8}{4}$

9. $\dfrac{9}{13}$ ☐ $\dfrac{2}{13}$ 10. $\dfrac{3}{5}$ ☐ $\dfrac{2}{5}$

Write the decimal equivalent of the fractions.

1. $\dfrac{1}{3}$ 2. $\dfrac{5}{11}$ 3. $\dfrac{6}{15}$ 4. $\dfrac{4}{5}$ 5. $\dfrac{7}{8}$ 6. $\dfrac{3}{7}$ 7. 1/5

8. $\dfrac{1}{2}$ 9. $\dfrac{3}{4}$ 10. $\dfrac{6}{7}$ 11. $\dfrac{1}{8}$ 12. $\dfrac{3}{20}$ 13. $\dfrac{7}{21}$ 14. $\dfrac{3}{28}$ 15. $\dfrac{4}{32}$

Order the fractions from least to greatest.

1. $\dfrac{1}{2},\dfrac{1}{3},\dfrac{1}{4}$ 2. $\dfrac{1}{2},\dfrac{3}{5},\dfrac{1}{20}$ 3. $\dfrac{3}{7},\dfrac{4}{7},\dfrac{1}{7}$ 4. $\dfrac{3}{7},\dfrac{1}{49},\dfrac{2}{7}$ 5. $\dfrac{7}{8},\dfrac{2}{8},\dfrac{3}{8}$

6. $\dfrac{4}{5},\dfrac{7}{5},\dfrac{2}{5}$ 7. $\dfrac{1}{4},\dfrac{2}{8},\dfrac{1}{2}$ 8. $\dfrac{5}{6},\dfrac{1}{5},\dfrac{3}{4}$ 9. $\dfrac{1}{6},\dfrac{6}{7},\dfrac{3}{4}$ 10. $\dfrac{4}{5},\dfrac{1}{5},\dfrac{2}{15}$

Order the fractions from greatest to least.

1. $\dfrac{1}{2},\dfrac{1}{3},\dfrac{1}{4}$ 2. $\dfrac{1}{2},\dfrac{3}{5},\dfrac{1}{20}$ 3. $\dfrac{3}{7},\dfrac{4}{7},\dfrac{1}{7}$ 4. $\dfrac{3}{7},\dfrac{1}{49},\dfrac{2}{7}$ 5. $\dfrac{7}{8},\dfrac{2}{8},\dfrac{3}{8}$

6. $\dfrac{4}{5},\dfrac{7}{5},\dfrac{2}{5}$ 7. $\dfrac{1}{4},\dfrac{2}{8},\dfrac{1}{2}$ 8. $\dfrac{5}{6},\dfrac{1}{5},\dfrac{3}{4}$ 9. $\dfrac{1}{6},\dfrac{6}{7},\dfrac{3}{4}$ 10. $\dfrac{4}{5},\dfrac{1}{5},\dfrac{2}{15}$

Order the fractions from least to greatest and from greatest to least.

1. $\dfrac{3}{2},\dfrac{3}{8},\dfrac{1}{4}$ 2. $\dfrac{1}{3},\dfrac{2}{1},\dfrac{3}{4}$ 3. $\dfrac{2}{3},\dfrac{2}{5},\dfrac{3}{4}$ 4. $\dfrac{2}{3},\dfrac{3}{5},\dfrac{4}{5}$

5. $\dfrac{4}{7},\dfrac{6}{3},\dfrac{4}{8}$ 6. $\dfrac{3}{4},\dfrac{2}{3},\dfrac{7}{12}$ 7. $\dfrac{5}{8},\dfrac{3}{5},\dfrac{2}{3}$ 8. $\dfrac{1}{5},\dfrac{1}{4},\dfrac{3}{4}$

9. $\dfrac{9}{3},\dfrac{2}{4},\dfrac{8}{2}$ 10. $\dfrac{4}{8},\dfrac{10}{5},\dfrac{8}{10}$

LESSON 3.3

ADDING AND SUBTRACTING FRACTIONS WITH THE SAME DENOMINATORS

Like fractions are fractions with the same denominators—for example, $\frac{5}{7}$ and $\frac{1}{7}$ are like fractions.

To add or subtract fractions with the same denominators, add or subtract the numerators, and then write the sum or difference over the common denominator.

Sample Work 1

Add $\frac{2}{5} + \frac{1}{5}$.

Solution

$$\frac{2}{5} + \frac{1}{5} = \frac{2+1}{5} \quad \longleftarrow \quad \text{add the numerators}$$

$$= \frac{3}{5}$$

Sample Work 2

Subtract $\frac{5}{8} - \frac{3}{8}$.

Solution

$$\frac{5}{8} - \frac{3}{8} = \frac{5-3}{8} \quad \longleftarrow \quad \text{subtract the numerators}$$

$$= \frac{2}{8}$$

Practice

Add.

1. $\frac{2}{3} + \frac{1}{3}$
2. $\frac{3}{7} + \frac{2}{7}$
3. $\frac{4}{9} + \frac{5}{9}$
4. $\frac{6}{8} + \frac{7}{8}$
5. $\frac{3}{6} + \frac{2}{6}$

6. $\frac{4}{7} + \frac{1}{7}$
7. $\frac{1}{11} + \frac{2}{11}$
8. $\frac{13}{15} + \frac{1}{15}$
9. $\frac{3}{17} + \frac{2}{17}$
10. $\frac{8}{13} + \frac{7}{13}$

11. $\frac{1}{4} + \frac{1}{4}$
12. $\frac{3}{5} + \frac{2}{5}$
13. $\frac{7}{14} + \frac{7}{14}$
14. $\frac{5}{11} + \frac{5}{11}$

15. Sarah added $\frac{3}{5}$ cup of cayenne pepper and $\frac{1}{5}$ cup of garlic pepper as parts of a trail mix recipe. How many cups of pepper did Sarah add in all?

16. Jabateh drinks $\frac{5}{9}$ glass of water in the afternoon and $\frac{7}{9}$ glass in the evening. How much water does Jabateh drink in all?

17. Last Sunday, Paul watered his cabbage garden with $\frac{1}{9}$ bucket of water. Four hours later, he added another $\frac{1}{9}$ bucket. How much water did Paul use to water his garden in all?

18. On Friday, it snowed $\frac{3}{7}$ inch. On Saturday, it snowed $\frac{1}{7}$ inch. What was the total amount of snowfall on the two days?

19. Nuwo poured $\frac{3}{11}$ gallon of water into a bucket. Later she added $\frac{1}{11}$ gallon more. How much water is in the bucket now?

20. Erica measured a red pole that was $\frac{3}{4}$ yard long. Then she measured another green pole that was $\frac{1}{4}$ yard long. How long was the two combined?

21. At lunchtime, Bomi's cafeteria serves $\frac{1}{5}$ pot of chicken soup and $\frac{1}{5}$ pot of onion soup. How many pots of soup will be served in all?

Subtract.

1. $\frac{7}{13} - \frac{7}{13}$
2. $\frac{5}{12} - \frac{3}{12}$
3. $\frac{4}{10} - \frac{2}{10}$
4. $\frac{3}{14} - \frac{1}{14}$
5. $\frac{6}{15} - \frac{5}{15}$

6. $\frac{3}{5} - \frac{2}{5}$
7. $\frac{50}{61} - \frac{40}{61}$
8. $\frac{8}{15} - \frac{4}{15}$
9. $\frac{7}{12} - \frac{5}{12}$
10. $\frac{3}{8} - \frac{1}{8}$

11. $\dfrac{2}{3} - \dfrac{1}{3}$ 12. $\dfrac{30}{40} - \dfrac{30}{40}$

13. Gongar bakes apple pies for his family's children party. The boys eat $\dfrac{5}{7}$ of the pie, and the girls eat $\dfrac{3}{7}$ of the pie. How much pie will the boys eat more than the girls?

14. Bunasua's history textbook weighs $\dfrac{4}{9}$ pound, and her science textbook weighs $\dfrac{2}{9}$ pound. How much more does the history textbook weigh than the science textbook?

15. A tailor cuts $\dfrac{5}{11}$ inch off a skirt and $\dfrac{1}{11}$ inch off a pair of pants. How much more does the tailor cut off the skirt than the pants?

16. Deowin and Meleh own wheat farms adjacent to each other. Deowin harvested $\dfrac{7}{10}$ acre of wheat on Friday. Meleh harvested $\dfrac{1}{10}$ acre. How many more acres did Deowin harvest than Meleh?

17. Makengbeh measured a red pole that was $\dfrac{3}{4}$ yard long. She later measured another green pole that was $\dfrac{1}{4}$ yard long. How much longer was the red pole than the green pole?

LESSON 3.4

ADDING AND SUBTRACTING FRACTIONS WITH DIFFERENT DENOMINATORS

To add or subtract fractions with different denominators, make the denominators the same and then add or subtract.

Sample Work 1

Add $\frac{3}{5} + \frac{1}{3}$.

Solution

$$\frac{3}{5} + \frac{1}{3} = \frac{9+5}{15} \longleftarrow \quad \text{5 and 3 can go into 15 without a remainder, so 15 is the common denominator for both fractions } (3 \times 5 = 15).$$

$$= \frac{14}{15}$$

Sample Work 2

Subtract $\frac{3}{4} - \frac{2}{5}$

Solution

$$\frac{3}{4} - \frac{2}{5} = \frac{15}{20} - \frac{8}{20} \longleftarrow \quad \text{4 and 5 can go into 20 without a remainder, so 20 is the common denominator for both fractions } (4 \times 5 = 20).$$

$$= \frac{7}{20}$$

Practice

Add.

1. $\frac{2}{5} + \frac{1}{4}$ 2. $\frac{3}{6} + \frac{5}{4}$ 3. $\frac{6}{2} + \frac{8}{7}$ 4. $\frac{1}{2} + \frac{3}{4}$ 5. $\frac{6}{8} + \frac{5}{9}$ 6. $\frac{1}{2} + \frac{2}{5}$

7. $\frac{2}{5} + \frac{3}{4}$ 8. $\frac{6}{7} + \frac{1}{21}$ 9. $\frac{7}{21} + \frac{1}{6}$ 10. $\frac{1}{9} + \frac{1}{8}$

11. Mr. Kaya traveled from Ibuja to Lagos on Tuesday. He traveled $\frac{3}{8}$ mile from 6:00 a.m. to 10:00 a.m. and $\frac{1}{4}$ mile from 11:00 a.m. to 1:30 p.m., reaching his destination in the afternoon. How far did Mr. Kaya travel in all?

12. Teresa makes her famous seafood gumbo, which she uses jumbo shrimp and blue crab, for lunch. Her recipe calls for $\frac{3}{7}$ pound of shrimp and $\frac{1}{5}$ pound of crab. How many total pounds of seafood does Teresa use in all?

Subtract.

13. $\frac{8}{5} - \frac{6}{9}$ 14. $\frac{1}{2} - \frac{1}{3}$ 15. $\frac{6}{8} - \frac{2}{3}$ 16. $\frac{4}{6} - \frac{3}{7}$ 17. $\frac{6}{8} - \frac{5}{9}$ 18. $\frac{7}{9} - \frac{1}{3}$

19. Bunasua's history book weighs $\frac{1}{3}$ pound, and his science book weighs $\frac{1}{9}$ pound. How much more does the history book weigh than the science book?

20. Kona filled a bucket with $\frac{9}{11}$ gallon of oil. Two hours later, he realized only $\frac{1}{4}$ gallon of oil remained in the bucket. How much oil leaked out of the bucket?

21. Johnson walked $\frac{5}{9}$ mile and ran $\frac{2}{7}$ mile. How much farther did Johnson walk than run?

LESSON 3.5

ADDING AND SUBTRACTING MIXED NUMBERS WITH LIKE AND UNLIKE DENOMINATORS

Mixed fractions are fractions with whole numbers. For example, $3\frac{1}{2}$, $1\frac{2}{3}$, and $3\frac{5}{6}$ are mixed fractions. The fraction $3\frac{5}{6}$ is read as "three and five-sixths."

Sample Work 1

Add and write the answer in mixed numbers $1\frac{1}{3} + 2\frac{1}{3}$.

Solution

$1\frac{1}{3} + 2\frac{1}{3}$ ⟵ like denominator

$$1\frac{1}{3} + 2\frac{1}{3} = \frac{4}{3} + \frac{7}{3}$$ ⟵ change to improper fractions

$$= \frac{4+7}{3}$$ ⟵ add the numerators

$$= \frac{11}{3}$$

$$= 3\frac{2}{3}$$

Sample Work 2

Add $4\frac{1}{2} + 3\frac{1}{4}$. Write your answer as an improper fraction.

Solution

$$4\frac{1}{2} + 3\frac{1}{4} \quad \longleftarrow \quad \text{unlike denominator}$$

$$4\frac{1}{2} + 3\frac{1}{4} = \frac{9}{2} + \frac{13}{4}$$

$$= \frac{18+13}{4}$$

$$= \frac{31}{4}$$

Sample Work 3

Subtract $2\frac{3}{4} - 1\frac{1}{4}$.

Solution

$$2\frac{3}{4} - 1\frac{1}{4} = \frac{11}{4} - \frac{5}{4}$$

$$= \frac{11-5}{4}$$

$$= \frac{6}{4}$$

Sample Work 4

Subtract and write the answer in mixed numbers $5\frac{3}{4} - 2\frac{3}{7}$.

Solution

$$5\frac{3}{4} - 2\frac{3}{7} = \frac{23}{4} - \frac{17}{7}$$

$$= \frac{161-68}{28}$$

$$= \frac{93}{28}$$

$$= 3\frac{9}{28}$$

Practice

Add.

1. $2\frac{3}{6} + 1\frac{4}{6}$ 2. $4\frac{2}{4} + 2\frac{1}{4}$ 3. $3\frac{1}{8} + 4\frac{2}{8}$ 4. $5\frac{2}{4} + 1\frac{3}{7}$

5. $6\frac{4}{10} + 1\frac{3}{4}$ 6. $3\frac{1}{5} + 7\frac{1}{6}$

7. The Cody family spent $\frac{1}{4}$ hour driving to the store. Then they spent $2\frac{3}{4}$ hours shopping and checking out. How long did the Cody family spend all together driving to the store and then shopping and checking out?

8. A weather forecaster at Bong Community College recorded the rainfall in Sanoyae in three consecutive months. In May, he recorded $1\frac{1}{5}$ inches of rainfall. In June, he recorded $2\frac{1}{5}$ inches of rainfall. In July, he recorded $\frac{3}{5}$ inch of rainfall. What was the total amount of rainfall the weather forecaster recorded during the three months?

9. Luci had a blue extension cord that was $7\frac{2}{9}$ feet long and a cream extension cord that was $5\frac{3}{9}$ feet long. If Luci plugged one extension cord into the other, how far did the cords reach?

10. On Wednesday, Kehnel drives to the store and uses $1\frac{1}{11}$ gallons of gasoline. On Thursday, she drives to the casino and uses $2\frac{1}{11}$ gallons of gasoline. How much gasoline will Kehnel use in all?

11. Liza measures a piece of iron that is $2\frac{1}{4}$ feet long and glues it to another piece of iron that is $1\frac{1}{4}$ feet long. Together, how long are the two pieces of iron?

12. A cafeteria manager orders $6\frac{1}{3}$ pounds of brown sugar and $7\frac{2}{3}$ pounds of white sugar. How many pounds of sugar does the manager order in all?

Subtract.

13. $10\frac{3}{5} - 6\frac{1}{5}$ 14. $11\frac{4}{8} - 5\frac{3}{8}$ 15. $9\frac{2}{3} - 5\frac{1}{3}$ 16. $11\frac{5}{10} - 7\frac{3}{8}$

17. $32\frac{1}{6} - 10\frac{9}{10}$

18. Meko cuts an electric wire into two pieces. The first piece is $7\frac{5}{13}$ centimeters long. The second piece is $5\frac{2}{13}$ centimeters long. How long is the wire that Meko started with? Write your answer as a whole or mixed number.

19. Six months ago, Nancy grew $2\frac{2}{3}$ inches. Her sister grew $1\frac{1}{3}$ inches. How much more did Nancy grow than her sister? Write your answer as an improper fraction.

20. Red River Zoo has two elephants. The female elephant weighs $3\frac{6}{7}$ tons. The male elephant weighs $1\frac{5}{7}$ tons. How much more does the female elephant weigh than the male elephant?

21. This morning, James started the day with $13\frac{7}{9}$ buckets of corn seeds. After spending the morning sowing seeds, he now has $6\frac{2}{9}$ buckets left. How many buckets of seeds did James sow? Write your answer as a mixed number.

22. Gbekugbeh and Saywala weigh their pet dogs. Gbekugbeh's dog weighs $13\frac{3}{7}$ pounds. Saywala's dog weighs $5\frac{1}{7}$ pounds. How much more does Gbekugbeh's dog weigh than Saywala's dog?

MULTIPLYING AND DIVIDING FRACTIONS WITH MIXED NUMBERS

Sample Work 1

Multiply $3\frac{1}{2} \times 2\frac{3}{4}$.

Solution

$$3\frac{1}{2} \times 2\frac{3}{4} = \frac{7}{2} \times \frac{11}{4} \text{ changed to improper fractions}$$

$$= \frac{7 \times 11}{2 \times 4} \quad \text{multiplying numerators by numerators and denominators by denominators}$$

$$= \frac{77}{8}$$

Sample Work 2

Multiply and write the answer in mixed numbers $1\frac{1}{5} \times 4\frac{1}{2}$.

Solution

$$1\frac{1}{5} \times 4\frac{1}{2} = \frac{6}{5} \times \frac{9}{2}$$

$$= \frac{6 \times 9}{5 \times 2}$$

$$= \frac{54}{10}$$

$$= 5\frac{4}{10}$$

Sample Work 3

Divide $3\frac{1}{4} \div 3\frac{1}{4}$.

Solution

$$3\frac{1}{4} \div 3\frac{1}{4} = \frac{13}{4} \div \frac{13}{4} \qquad \text{changed to improper fractions}$$

$$= \frac{13}{4} \times \frac{4}{13} \qquad \text{inverted the second fraction and changed the sign of operation to multiplication sign}$$

$$= \frac{1}{1} \times \frac{1}{1}$$

$$= \frac{1 \times 1}{1 \times 1}$$

$$= \frac{1}{1}$$

$$= 1$$

Sample Work 4

Divide $2\frac{3}{2} \div 3\frac{1}{4}$.

Solution

$$2\frac{3}{2} \div 3\frac{1}{4} = \frac{7}{2} \div \frac{13}{4}$$

$$= \frac{7}{2} \times \frac{4}{13}$$

$$= \frac{7 \times 4}{2 \times 13}$$

$$= \frac{28}{26}$$

$$= \frac{14}{13} \text{ or } 1\frac{1}{13}$$

Practice

Multiply.

1. $7\frac{3}{4} \times 2\frac{5}{4}$

2. $10\frac{4}{8} \times 6\frac{2}{8}$

3. $24\frac{6}{2} \times 30\frac{1}{2}$

4. $10 \times 8\frac{2}{3}$

5. $4\frac{1}{3} \times 3\frac{2}{4}$

6. $8\frac{1}{7} \times 1\frac{5}{15}$

Divide.

7. $1\frac{1}{3} \div 4\frac{8}{3}$

8. $4\frac{2}{8} \div 2\frac{5}{8}$

9. $1\frac{0}{4} \div 2\frac{0}{4}$

10. $1\frac{1}{3} \div 6$

11. $8\frac{5}{7} \div 4\frac{1}{3}$

12. $2\frac{1}{4} \div 10\frac{0}{2}$

UNIT 4
MEASUREMENT

Learning Points

In this unit, we shall

- add and subtract units of measures; and
- find perimeters and areas of polygons.

LESSON 4.1

READING UNITS OF MEASURES—ENGLISH SYSTEM

Read the following measurement tables.

Length

12 inches (in) = 1 foot (ft)

36 inches (in) = 1 yard (yd)

36 inches (in) = 3 feet (ft)

3 feet (ft) = 1 yard (yd)

16.5 feet (ft) = 1 rod (rd)

5,280 feet (ft) = 1 mile (mi)

Volume

16 ounces (oz) = 1 pint (pt)

2 pints (pt) = 1 quart (qt)

4 quarts (qt) = 1 gallon (gal)

Weight

16 ounces (oz) = 1 pound (lb)

2,000 pounds (lb) = 1 ton

Time

60 seconds (sec) = 1 minute (min)

MANPEKIN

60 minutes (min) = 1 hour (hr)

24 hours (hr) = 1 day

7 days (da) = 1 week (wk)

365 days (da) = 1 year

52 weeks (wk) = 1 year

12 months (mon) = 1 year (yr)

Sample Work 1

State the abbreviation for second.

Solution

The students state the abbreviation according to class discussion and established rule, sec.

Sample Work 2

Write the abbreviation for minute.

Solution

Minute = min

Sample Work 3

Write the abbreviation for pounds.

Solution

pounds = lbs

Sample Work 4

Write the abbreviation for ounces.

Solution

ounces = oz

Practice

Write the abbreviation for each unit of measurements.

1. gallon	2. yard	3. feet	4. inch	5. week
6. year	7. pint	8. mile	9. hour	10. quart

LESSON 4.2

ADDING UNITS OF MEASURES—ENGLISH SYSTEM

We can add units of measures just as in the case of whole numbers.

Sample Work 1

Add 12 inches (in) + 12 inches (in).

Solution

12 inches (in) + 12 inches (in) = 24 inches or = 2 feet

Sample Work 2

Add 7 days + 7 days.

Solution

7 days + 7 days = 7days
$\quad\quad\quad\quad\quad$ + 7days
$\quad\quad\quad\quad\quad\quad$ 14 days or 2 weeks

Sample Work 3

Add 60 minutes (min) + 30 minutes (min).

Solution

$\quad$ 60 minutes (min)
+30 minutes (min)
$\quad$ 90 minutes (min) or 1 hr 30 min

Sample Work 4

Add 6 quarts (qt) + 2 quarts (qt).

Solution

    6 quarts (qt)
  +2 quarts (qt)
    8 quarts (qt) or 2 gallons

Practice

Add and discuss.

1. 11 oz + 5 oz   2. 3 pt + 1 pt   3. 4 ft + 2 ft   4. 3 yd + 2 yd   5. 3 min + 1 min

6. 40 sec + 20 sec   7. 16 in + 8 in   8. 90 da + 30 da   9. 47 wk + 5 wk

10. 315 da + 50 da   11. 14 da + 2 wk   12. 1 yr + 12 mon   13. 2 yr + 24 mon   14. 12 in + 1 ft

15. 30 min + 30 min   16. 44 min + 16 min   17. 24 hr + 2 da   18. 2 yr + 12 mon   19. 52 wk + 365 da

20. 4 wk + 4 mon   21. 50 sec + 40 sec   22. 25 sec + 35 sec 23. 90 min + 30 min 24. 20 in + 16 in

25. 9 ft + 3 ft   26. 10 yd + 2 yd

LESSON 4.3

SUBTRACTING UNITS OF MEASURES—ENGLISH SYSTEM

We can also subtract units of measures.

Sample Work 1

Subtract
$$
\begin{array}{r}
96 \text{ minutes (min)} \\
-\underline{36 \text{ minutes (min)}} \\
60 \text{ minutes (min) or 1 hr}
\end{array}
$$

Sample Work 2

Subtract
$$
\begin{array}{r}
120 \text{ seconds (sec)} \\
-\underline{90 \text{ seconds (sec)}} \\
30 \text{ seconds (sec)}
\end{array}
$$

Sample Work 3

Subtract
$$
\begin{array}{r}
50 \text{ gallons (gal} \\
-\underline{35 \text{ gallons (gal)}} \\
15 \text{ gallons (gal)}
\end{array}
$$

Sample Work 4

Subtract
$$
\begin{array}{r}
72 \text{ inches (in)} \\
-\underline{24 \text{ inches (in)}} \\
48 \text{ inches (in) or 4 feet}
\end{array}
$$

Practice

Subtract and discuss.

1. 2,800 feet (ft)
    -2,480 feet (ft)

2. 49.5 feet (ft)
    -16.5 feet (ft)

3. 72 hours (hr)
    -24 hours (hr)

4. 24 quarts (qt)
    -14 quarts (qt)

5. 60 pints (pt) of milk
    -20 pints (pt) of milk

6. 3 tons of rice
    -1 ton of rice

7. 35 days (da)
    -21 days (da)

8. 180 seconds (sec)
    -60 seconds (sec)

9. 80 ounces
    -32 ounces

10. 730.0 days (da)
    -182.5 days (da)

11. 50 sec - 40 sec   12. 120 sec - 60 sec   13. 90 min - 30 min   14. 20 in - 8 in   15. 9 ft - 3 ft

16. 56 da – 14 da   17. 48 mon - 12 mon

LESSON 4.4

FINDING PERIMETERS AND AREAS OF SQUARES

A square is a rectangle with four sides and angles. All the four sides are equal. All four angles are equal.

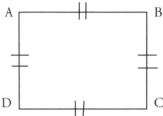

Sides AB, BC, CD, and DA are equal.

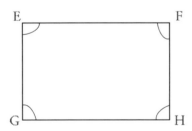

Angles E, F, G, and H are equal.

Formulas for Finding the Perimeter and Area of a Square

Perimeter (P) = 4 x S = S + S + S + S, i. e. add all the four sides. Note: S = side

$$P = 4 \times S$$

Area (A) = S x S

Sample Work 1

If S = 2 feet, find P.

Solution

P = S + S + S + S

P = 2 feet + 2 feet + 2 feet + 2 feet

P = 4 feet + 4 feet

P = 8 feet (ft)

Sample Work 2

Solve Sample Work 1 using P = 4 x S.

Solution

P = 4 x S

S = 2 ft

P = 4 x 2 ft

p = 8 feet (ft)

Sample Work 3

Each side of a square box is 6 inches. Find the perimeter of the box.

Solution

P = S + S + S + S

S = 6 inches

P = 6 in + 6 in + 6 in + 6 in

P = 12 in + 12 in

P = 24 inches (in)

Sample Work 4

Each side of a square potato green garden is 4 feet. Find the area.

Solution

A= S x S

    A= 4 ft x 4 ft

    A = 16 ft²

    A = 16 sq ft

Notice that area is measured in square unit.

Sample Work 5

Each side of a square cabbage farm is 31 yards. Find the area.

Solution

    A = S x S

    A= 31 yd x 31 yd

    A = 961 yd²

    A = 961 sq yd

Practice

Find the perimeter of a square beans garden if each side of the garden is given as follows.

    Use P = 4S or P = S + S + S + S

1. S = 10 feet	2. S = 15 feet	3. S = 30 feet	4. S = 9 yards
5. S = 11 inches	6. S = 8 yards	7. S = 20 inches	8. S = 14 feet
9. S = 25 inches	10. S = 13 yards	11. S = 12 feet	12. S = 8 feet
13. S = 10 inches	14. S = 17 yards	15. S = 13 feet	16. S = 15 meters
17. S = 5 meters	18. S = 13 centimeters	19. S = 32 centimeters	20. S = 40 meters

Find the area of a square house if each side of the house measures as follows. Use $A = S^2$ or $A = S \times S$.

1. S = 10 in	2. S = 5 in	3. S = 6 in	4. S = 9 ft
5. S = 12 ft	6. S = 13 ft	7. S = 14 ft	8. S = 11 yd
9. S = 12 yd	10. S = 26 yd	11. S = 52 in	12. S = 10 cm
13. S = 9 m	14. S = 15 cm	15. S = 11 m	16. S = 28 m
17. S = 16 cm	18. S = 37 cm	19. S = 21 cm	20. S = 72 in

LESSON 4.5

FINDING PERIMETERS AND AREAS OF RECTANGLES

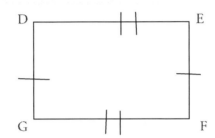 A rectangle has four sides. The two opposite sides are equal. The two opposite sides are parallel.

The formula for finding perimeter of a rectangle is, perimeter (P) = 2 x length (l) + 2 x width (w).

$$P = 2l + 2w \text{ or } 2 \times l + 2 \times w$$

The formula for finding area of a rectangle is, area (A) = length (l) x width (w).

$$A = l \times w$$

Sample Work 1

The length of a rectangle is 5 feet, and the width is 3 feet. Find the perimeter and the area.

Solution

Perimeter (P) = 2 x l + 2 x w

= 2 x 5 feet + 2 x 3 feet

= 10 ft + 6 ft

= 16 ft

Area (A) = l x w

= 5 ft x 3 ft

= 15 sq ft or 15 ft^2

Sample Work 2

If l = 6 in and w = 4 in, find the perimeter and the area.

Solution

P = 2 x l + 2 x w

= 2 x 6 in + 2 x 4 in

= 12 in + 8 in

= 20 in

A = l x w

= 6 in x 4 in

= 24 in^2 or 24 sq in

Practice

I. Find the perimeter of a rectangular football field with the given lengths and widths. Use P = 2 x l + 2 x w.

1. l = 10 feet, w = 8 feet   2. l = 6 yards, w = 4 yards   3. l = 25 feet, w = 20 feet

4. l = 30 feet, w = 26 feet   5. l = 9 feet, w = 8 feet   6. l = 22 feet, w = 18 feet

7. l = 15 feet, w = 12 feet

8.   5 in

4 in

9.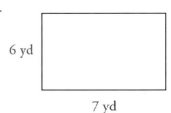

6 yd

7 yd

10.

8 ft

11 ft

II.   Dio has twenty estate houses in Zwedru City, which are all built in rectangular shapes. The lengths and widths of the houses are measured as follows. Find the area occupied by each estate house.

Use A = l × w.

1.   l = 5 feet, w = 3 feet

2.   l = 35 feet, w = 23 feet

3.   l = 6 feet, w = 4 feet

4.   l = 8 feet, w = 7 feet

5.   l = 5 cm, w = 3 cm

6.   l = 10 inches, w = 9 inches

7.   l = 18 m, w = 15 m

8.   l = 11 yards, w = 8 yards

9.   l = 30 yards, w = 20 yards

10.   l = 12 yards, w = 10 yards

11.   l = 3 yards, w = 2 yards

12.   l = 13 yards, w = 11 yards

13.   l = 20 cm, w = 12 cm

14.   l = 8 ft, w = 4 ft

15.   l = 10 yd, w = 9 yd

16.   l = 3 ft, w = 2 ft

17.   l = 7 cm, w = 3 cm

18.   l = 6 m, w = 5 m

19.   l = 36 m, w = 24 m

20.   l = 7 yd, w = 5 yd

LESSON 4.6

FINDING PERIMETERS AND AREAS OF TRIANGLES

I.

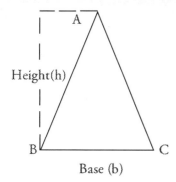

II.

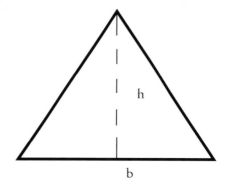

Triangles are used in many construction industries—for example, building and road. Engineers use triangles to design building roofs. These diagrams, I and II, are triangles.

Use the following formulas to find the perimeter and area of a triangle.

Perimeter (P) = a + b + c ⟵—————— add the three sides of the triangle

$$P = a + b + c$$

Area (A) = $\frac{1}{2}$ x base x height

$$A = \frac{1}{2}b \times h$$

$$A = \frac{1}{2}bh$$

Sample Work 1

If the height (h) of a triangle is 22 feet and the base (b) is 6 feet, find the area.

Solution

Area (A) = $\frac{1}{2}$ x base (b) x height (h)

$A = \frac{1}{2}b \times h$

$A = \frac{1}{2} \times 6 \text{ ft} \times 22 \text{ ft}$

$A = \frac{1}{2} \times 132 \text{ ft}^2$

$A = 66 \text{ ft}^2 \text{ or } 66 \text{ sq ft}$

Sample Work 2

If b = 3 yd and h = 4 yd, find A.

Solution

$A = \frac{1}{2}bh = \frac{1}{2} \times 3 \text{ yd} \times 4 \text{ yd}$

$A = \frac{1}{2} \times 12 \text{ yd}^2$

$A = 6 \text{ yd}^2 \text{ or } 6 \text{ sq yd}$

Sample Work 3

Find the perimeter of the triangle.

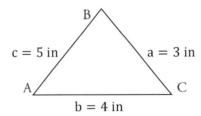

Solution

$P = a + b + c$

$= 3 \text{ in} + 4 \text{ in} + 5 \text{ in}$

$= 12 \text{ in}$

Sample Work 4

If $a = 6$ ft, $b = 7$ ft, and $c = 8$ft, find P.

Solution

$a = 6$ ft, $b = 7$ ft, $c = 8$ft

$P = a + b + c$

$= 6 \text{ ft} + 7 \text{ ft} + 8 \text{ ft}$

$= 6 \text{ ft} + 15 \text{ ft}$

$= 21 \text{ ft}$

Practice

If the sides $(a, b, \text{ and } c)$ of triangles are given as indicated, find the perimeter of each triangle. Use $P = a + b + c$.

1. $a = 2$ in, $b = 3$ in, $c = 4$ in

2. $a = 5$ in, $b = 6$ in, $c = 7$ in

3. $a = 8$ ft, $b = 9$ ft, $c = 10$ ft

4. $a = 3$ ft, $b = 4$ ft, $c = 5$ ft

5. $a = 1$ ft, $b = 2$ ft, $c = 3$ ft

6. $a = 7$ yd, $b = 5$ yd, $c = 10$ yd

7. $a = 10$ ft, $b = 8$ ft, $c = 7$ ft

8. $a = 3$ ft, $b = 8$ ft, $c = 8$ ft

9. $a= 15$ in, $b = 20$ in, $c = 25$ in

10. $a = 13$ in, $b = 12$ in, $c = 14$ in

11. $a = 16$ yd, $b = 18$ yd, $c = 19$ yd

12. $a = 10$ ft, $b = 15$ ft, $c = 20$ ft

Find the area (A) of a triangle with the given bases and heights. Use $A = \frac{1}{2} \times b \times h$.

1. b = 2 ft, h = 4 ft

2. b = 6 ft, h = 7 ft

3. b = 8 ft, h = 9 ft

4. b = 10 ft, h = 20 ft

5. b = 16 yd, h = 30 yd

6. b = 18 in, h = 20 in

7. b = 12 yd, h = 10 yd

8. b = 8 in, h = 12 in

9. b = 15 in, h = 12 in

10. b = 16 ft, h = 12 ft

11. b = 10 yd, h = 18 yd

12. b = 4 yd, h = 10 yd

13. b = 7 ft, h = 10 ft

14. b = 8 in, h = 9 in

FINDING PERIMETERS OF PARALLELOGRAMS

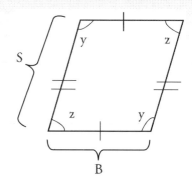

Properties of a parallelogram

4-sided shape

  Opposite sides equal in length

  Opposite sides parallel

  Opposite angles are equal. Angles "y" are the same
  and angles "z" are the same

A parallelogram is a four-sided shape with opposite sides parallel and equal in length.

Formula for Finding the Perimeter of a Parallelogram

Perimeter $(P) = 2(b + s)$ ⟵——— add the two adjacent sides

Or $P = 2b + 2s$

Sample Work 1

Find the perimeter of the parallelogram if b = 15 in and s = 10 in.

Solution

$P = 2(b + s)$

$P = 2(15 \text{ in} + 10 \text{ in})$

$P = 2(25 \text{ in})$

$P = 50 \text{ in}$

Sample Work 2

Find the perimeter of the parallelogram with b and s shown.

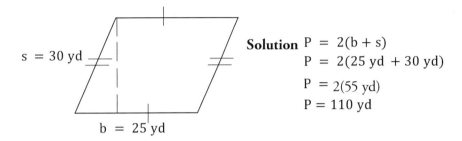

s = 30 yd

b = 25 yd

Solution P = 2(b + s)

P = 2(25 yd + 30 yd)

P = 2(55 yd)

P = 110 yd

Practice

Find the perimeter of the parallelograms as shown below. Use $P = 2(b + s)$.

1.

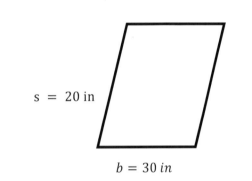

s = 20 in

b = 30 in

2.

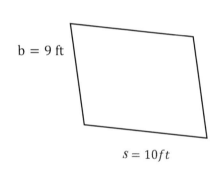

b = 9 ft

s = 10ft

3.

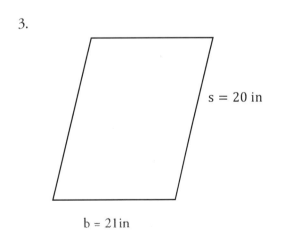

s = 20 in

b = 21 in

4.

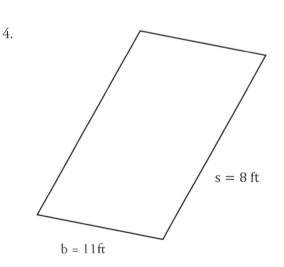

s = 8 ft

b = 11 ft

5.

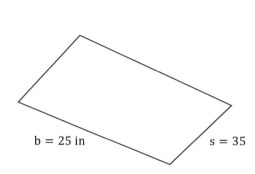

b = 25 in   s = 35

6.

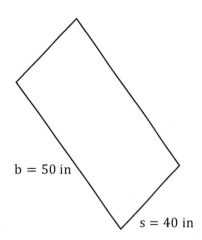

b = 50 in   s = 40 in

7.   Draw a parallelogram and give three properties.

UNIT 5

GEOMETRY

Learning Points

In this unit, we shall

- define, identify, and measure angles;
- classify triangles by sides and angles;
- classify quadrilaterals; and
- find dimensions of a circle.

LESSON 5.1

MEASURING ANGLES

Some key words used in measuring an angle are point, line, and ray.

A *point* looks like this: .   .   .

A *line* looks like this: ←—————————→

A line is a straight and continuous collection of points that goes on continuously in opposite directions. It has no end points.

This represents line AB: $\overleftrightarrow{AB}$

A *ray* looks like this:

···→

Ray $\overrightarrow{AB}$: This means the line that starts from point A. A ray has one end point, and it goes on and on in one direction.

An angle is made by two rays having the same end point. The end point is called vertex.

two rays, A and B, forming an angle at the vertex, C

Vertex

Angles are measured in degree, minute, or second.

One complete rotation is an angle of 360 degrees.

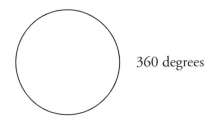

360 degrees

Types of Angles and Their Classifications

A straight angle is 180 degrees.

A right angle is 90 degrees.

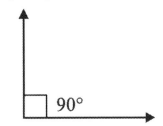

The two rays meet at 90 degrees.

An acute angle measures greater than 0^0 and less than 90^0.

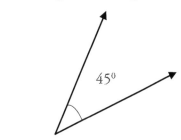

45^0

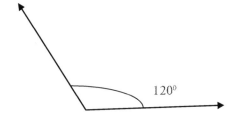

120^0

An obtuse angle measures greater than 90 degrees and less than 180 degrees.

Practice

1. Draw two rays to form an angle.

2. Draw two rays that meet at 90 degrees.

3. Draw a 180-degree angle.

4. Draw a line.

5. Draw a ray.

6. Draw an obtuse angle.

7. Angles are measured in degrees: true or false.

8. Draw a right angle.

9. An obtuse angle measures greater than 90 degrees but less than 180 degrees: true or false.

LESSON 5.2

CLASSIFYING QUADRILATERALS BY SIDES AND ANGLES

This figure represents a quadrilateral.

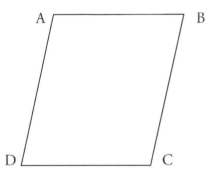

It is a polygon. It has four sides.

Some special types of quadrilaterals are:

Parallelogram

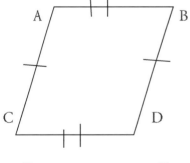

Properties:
It has two pairs of opposite sides.
   The two opposite sides are equal.
The two opposite sides are parallel.
   It has four angles.

Rectangle

It has two pairs of opposite sides.

The two opposite sides are equal.
The two opposite sides are parallel.
It has four right angles. All four angles are equal.

Square

S _____ R
| |
| |
P   Q

Trapezoid

N _____ M
K   L

It has four angles, all equal.
It has two pairs of opposite sides. It has four sides.
All the four sides are equal.
It has four right angles.

It has only one pair of opposite sides that are parallel.

Practice

1. List two properties of trapezoids.

2. List two properties of parallelograms.

3. List three properties of rectangles.

4. List four properties of squares.

5. Draw a rectangle.

6. Draw a square and give any two descriptions you know about it.

7. A trapezoid has four equal sides: true or false. If false, explain.

8. A square has four equal sides: true or false. If false, explain.

9. A parallelogram has three equal sides: true or false. If false, explain.

10. Give two similarities between a square and a rectangle.

11. Give two similarities between a parallelogram and a rectangle.

12. Show two differences between a parallelogram and a rectangle.

13. Show two differences between a square and a rectangle.

14. Show two differences between a square and a parallelogram.

LESSON 5.3

CLASSIFYING TRIANGLES BY SIDES AND ANGLES

A figure like this is called a triangle.

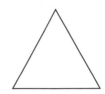

General properties:
    It has three sides.
    It has three angles.

Types of Triangles

Right Triangle

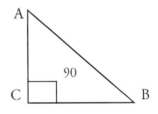

It has one right angle.

Equilateral Triangle

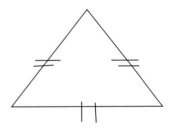

It has three sides, all equal.
    It has three angles.
    All three angles are equal, measuring 60 degrees each.

Isosceles Triangle

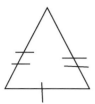

Two sides are equal. Two angles are equal.

Scalene Triangle

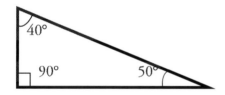

No sides are equal. No angles are equal.

90° - 50° - 40° is a scalene triangle since all the angles are different measures.

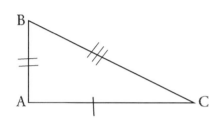

60° - 60° - 60° is not a scalene triangle since all the angles measures are not different.

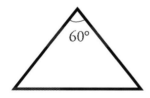

90° - 45° - 45° is an isosceles triangle since two angles are measured the same.

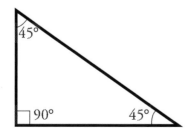

Practice

1. List two properties of a scalene triangle.

2. List two properties of an isosceles triangle.

3. List three properties of an equilateral triangle.

4. List two properties of a right triangle.

5. Draw an isosceles triangle. List one property.

6. Draw an equilateral triangle. Give any three descriptions you know about it.

LESSON 5.4

LINE SEGMENTS AND PARALLEL AND PERPENDICULAR LINES

Parallel lines do not have any point in common. The symbol | | is used to represent parallel lines. Parallel lines are always the same distance apart from each other. Parallel lines never intersect each other, no matter how much they extend in both directions. For example:

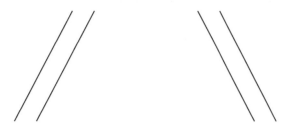

Line segment (AB) means a line from point A to point B. A line segment has two end points.

Perpendicular lines form right (90-degree) angles when they intersect. They are intersecting lines that always cross at one point. The symbol "⊥" is used to represent perpendicular lines. If one line is perpendicular to another, they must cross each other. Not only do perpendicular lines intersect, they also form equal 90-degree angles. Perpendicular lines intersect at a right angle. For example:

Generally, two lines can either be parallel or cross each other. For example:

Practice

1. Parallel lines never intersect: true or false. Show work.

2. Perpendicular lines intersect at a 90-degree angle: true or false. Show work.

3. Perpendicular lines form four 90-degree angles: true or false. Show work.

4. Draw two intersecting lines.

5. Draw two lines that are parallel to each other.

6. Draw two perpendicular lines.

7. Intersecting lines cross each other at one point: true or false. Show work.

FINDING CIRCUMFERENCE, DIAMETER, AND RADIUS OF A CIRCLE

A circle is a shape with all points having the same distance from the center. A circle is named by the center. For example, Circle A is as shown here:

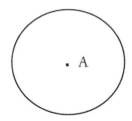

This is called Circle A since the center is at point A. The distance around the circle is called circumference.

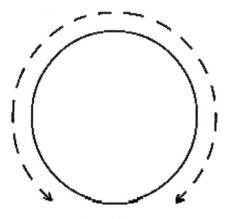

Circumference

A summary of a circle

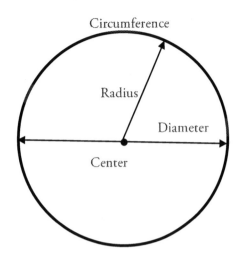

The formula for finding the circumference of a circle is, C = π d, where C = circumference, d = diameter, and π = 3.14.

Pi (π) is the ratio of the circumference of a circle to the diameter.

Sample Work 1

The diameter of a circle is 3 centimeters. What is the circumference?

Solution

C = π x d

C = 3.14 x 3 cm

C = 9.42 cm

Sample Work 2

Find the circumference of the circle whose diameter is 5 feet.

Solution

C = π x d

C = 3.14 x 5 ft

C = 15.7 ft

Sample Work 3

What is the circumference of a circle whose diameter is 3 yards?

Solution

$C = \pi \times d$

$C = 3.14 \times 3$ yd

$C = 9.42$ yd

A diameter is a line that divides a circle into two equal parts.

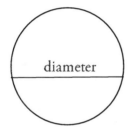

The formula for finding the diameter of a circle is, $D = 2 \times r$. D is the diameter, and r is the radius of the circle.

Sample Work 4

The radius of a circle is 2 inches. What is the diameter?

Solution

$D = 2r$

$D = 2 \times r$

$D = 2 \times 2$ in

$D = 4$ in

Sample Work 5

The circumference of a circle is 15.7 cm. What is the diameter?

Solution

$C = \pi \times d$

$15.7 \text{ cm} = 3.14 \times d$

$D = 15.7 \text{ cm} \div 3.14$

$D = 5 \text{ cm}$

Sample Work 6

Find the diameter of the circle whose radius is 8 feet.

Solution

$D = 2r$

$D = 2 \times 8 \text{ ft}$

$D = 16 \text{ ft}$

The radius of a circle is the distance from the center of a circle to any point of the circle.

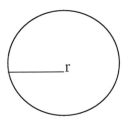

The formula for finding the radius of a circle is $r = \frac{d}{2}$, where r is the radius and d is the diameter.

Sample Work 7

Find the radius of the circle whose diameter is 14 feet.

Solution

$r = \dfrac{d}{2}$

$r = \dfrac{14}{2}\,\text{ft}$

$r = \dfrac{14}{2}\,\text{ft}$

$r = 7\ \text{ft}$

Sample Work 8

What is the radius of a circle whose diameter is 12 feet?

Solution

$r = \dfrac{d}{2}$

$r = \dfrac{12}{2}$

$r = \dfrac{12}{2}$

$r = 6\ \text{ft}$

Practice

1. The diameter of a circle is 2 centimeters. What is the circumference?

2. Find the circumference of the circle whose diameter is 10 feet.

3. What is the circumference of a circle whose diameter is 5 yards?

4. What is the diameter of a circle whose radius is 6 centimeters?

5. The radius of a circle is 14 inches. What is the diameter?

6. The circumference of a circle is 20 centimeters. What is the diameter?

7. Find the diameter of the circle whose radius is 18 feet.

8. Find the radius of the circle whose diameter is 22 meters.

9. What is the radius of a circle whose diameter is 16 centimeters?

10. Draw a circle and identify the circumference.

11. Draw a circle and identify the diameter.

12. Draw a circle and identify the radius.

13. Draw a circle and identify the center.

UNIT 6

RATIOS AND PROPORTIONS

Learning Points

In this unit, we shall

- identify and write ratio;
- identify and write proportion; and
- write ratio and proportion as a fraction.

LESSON 6.1

IDENTIFYING AND WRITING RATIOS

We use ratio to compare two things. For example, the ratio of males to females in a history class may be 3 to 4. We can write ratio in three different ways as follows: using a fraction, saying a number is to another number, or using a colon.

The way in which we write ratio tells which number or thing is to be in the denominator. The ratio of males to females in the history class is $\frac{3}{4}$ in fraction form.

Sample Work 1

Write the ratio in fraction and colon forms. Five third-grade students to ten students in all.

Solution

Fraction form: $\frac{5}{10}$ Colon form: 5:10

Sample Work 2

Write in words $\frac{3}{7}$.

Solution

3 to 7

Practice

Write each ratio as a fraction.

1. John has twenty goats. Five of the goats are males.

2. Tar buys thirty-five watermelons. Seven of the watermelons are spoiled.

3. 9 to 11

4. 5 to 7

5. 13 to 26

6. Five females to twenty-five males in a science class

7. $200 to $400

8. Five to thirty-three

Write each ratio in colon form.

9. John has twenty goats. Five of the goats are males.

10. Tar buys thirty-five watermelons. Seven of the watermelons are spoiled.

11. 9 to 11

12. 5 to 7

13. 13 to 26

14. Twenty-five males to five females in a science class

15. $200 to $400

16. Five to thirty-three

LESSON 6.2

IDENTIFYING AND WRITING PROPORTIONS

When two ratios are equal, it is called a proportion. We can write the cross product of a proportion. Double colons are used to show proportion. Two ratios are equal if their cross products are equal.

Sample Work 1

Write in colon form $\frac{3}{4} = \frac{9}{12}$.

Solution

$\frac{3}{4} = \frac{9}{12}$ is written in colon form as 3:4 :: 9:12.

This answer is read as 3 is to 4 as 9 is to 12.

Sample Work 2

Write in cross product form 3 is to 5 as 9 is to 15.

Solution

3 is to 5 as 9 is to 15 is written in cross product form as $\frac{3}{5} = \frac{9}{15}$.

Sample Work 3

Write the cross product: $\frac{2}{3} = \frac{6}{9}$.

Solution

Cross multiply.

2 x 9 = 3 x 6

18 = 18

The ratios are equal since the cross products are equal.

Practice

Write the cross products.

1. $\frac{1}{6} = \frac{5}{30}$ 2. $\frac{2}{3} = \frac{6}{9}$ 3. $\frac{4}{6} = \frac{8}{12}$ 4. $\frac{1}{3} = \frac{2}{6}$ 5. $\frac{1}{5} = \frac{2}{10}$ 6. $\frac{1}{4} = \frac{2}{8}$ 7. $\frac{2}{4} = \frac{4}{8}$

Write the proportion for each.

1. The ratio of 1 to 5 is the same as the ratio of 5 to 25.

2. The ratio of 1 to 4 is the same as the ratio of 4 to 16.

3. The ratio of 2 to 3 is the same as the ratio of 4 to 6.

4. The ratio of 2 to 3 is the same as the ratio of 6 to 9.

5. The ratio of 2 to 8 is the same as the ratio of 1 to 4.

6. The ratio of 2 to 10 is the same as the ratio of 1 to 5.

7. The ratio of 4 to 8 is the same as the ratio of 2 to 4.

8. The ratio of 1 to 2 is the same as the ratio of 9 to 18.

9. The ratio of 1 to 2 is the same as the ratio of 5 to10.

10. The ratio of 1 to 3 is the same as the ratio of 9 to 27.

11. Parwon spends thirty hours in two weeks to practice his negotiation skills. He practices forty-five hours in three weeks.

12. In the typing world, 80 words per minute is an acceptable skill. Then 2,400 words will be per 30 minutes.

13. In 2014, there were 3 deaths per 100 residents in the country. If there were 20,000 residents in the country during 2014, then 600 people died in 2014.

14. In 2018, 5 persons per 100 families graduated from high school in the county. If there were 10,000 families in the county during 2018, then 500 people graduated in 2018.

15. In the year 2000, there were 8 deaths per 1,000 residents in the district. If there were 2 million residents in the district during 2000, then 16,000 people died that year.

16. In a shipment of six hundred bags of rice, ten are found to be inedible. Fifteen inedible bags are expected to be in a shipment of nine hundred.

17. The ratio of girls to boys in a class is 6 to 5. If there are 300 boys in the class, then there are 360 girls.

WRITING PERCENT AS FRACTION AND DECIMAL

Learning Points

In this unit, we shall change percent to fraction, decimal, and vice versa.

LESSON 7.1

WRITING PERCENT AS FRACTION AND FRACTION AS PERCENT

In writing percent as a fraction, write the number before the percent sign as the numerator and express it over 100. For example, 7% is written in fraction as $\frac{7}{100}$.

The percent sign tells a denominator of 100. In other words, percent means hundredth.

Sample Work 1

Write 3% as a fraction.

Solution

$$3\% = \frac{3}{100}$$

Sample Work 2

Write 24% as a fraction.

Solution

$$24\% = \frac{24}{100}$$

Sample Work 3

Write 100% as a fraction.

Solution

$100\% = 100$ ⟵ drop the % sign

$= \dfrac{100}{100}$ ⟵ divide the number by 100

$= \dfrac{1}{1}$

$$100\% = 1$$

To write a fraction as a percent, multiply the fraction by 100 and then write a percent sign.

Sample Work 4

Write $\dfrac{1}{2}$ as percent.

Solution

$\dfrac{1}{2} = \dfrac{1}{2} \times 100$

$\dfrac{1}{2} \times \dfrac{100}{1}$

$= \dfrac{1 \times 100}{2 \times 1}$

$= \dfrac{100}{2}$ ⟵ divide by 2

$= 50$ ⟵ quotient

$= 50\%$ ⟵ write percent

Sample Work 5

Write $\dfrac{2}{5}$ as a percent.

Solution

$$\frac{2}{5} = \frac{2}{5} \times 100$$

$$= \frac{2}{5} \times \frac{100}{1}$$

$$= \frac{2 \times 100}{5 \times 1}$$

$$= \frac{200}{5} \longleftarrow \text{divide by 5}$$

$$= 40 \longleftarrow \text{quotient}$$

$$= 40\% \longleftarrow \text{write percent}$$

Sample Work 6

Write $\frac{9}{10}$ as percent.

Solution

$$\frac{9}{10} = 9 \div 10 \longleftarrow \text{divided by 10}$$

$$\frac{9}{10} = 9 \div 10$$

$$9 \div 10 = .9$$

$$= .9$$

Move the decimal point two places to the right.

$$= 90\% \longleftarrow \text{write percent}$$

Practice

Write the percent as a fraction.

1. 10% 2. 6% 3. 15% 4. 12% 5. 3% 6. 24% 7. 8% 8. 11% 9. 4%

10. 20% 11. 30% 12. 7% 13. 5% 14. 2% 15. 13% 16. 9% 17. 50% 18. 60%

19. 75% 20. 45%

Write the fraction as a percent.

1. $\frac{3}{2}$ 2. $\frac{5}{6}$ 3. $\frac{3}{5}$ 4. $\frac{4}{2}$ 5. $\frac{1}{5}$ 6. $\frac{2}{7}$ 7. $\frac{1}{4}$ 8. $\frac{10}{30}$ 9. $\frac{4}{8}$

10. $\frac{2}{6}$ 11. $\frac{1}{3}$ 12. $\frac{5}{2}$ 13. $\frac{6}{2}$ 14. $\frac{8}{2}$ 15. $\frac{7}{5}$ 16. $\frac{2}{9}$ 17. $\frac{1}{6}$ 18. $\frac{3}{9}$

LESSON 7.2

WRITING PERCENT AS DECIMAL AND DECIMAL AS PERCENT

To write percent as a decimal, divide the number before the percent sign by 100.

Sample Work 1

Write 25% as a decimal.

Solution

$25\% = \frac{25}{100}$ ◄——— number before % sign divided by 100

$= 0.25$

Another way to write percent as a decimal is to drop the percent sign and move the decimal point two places to the left.

Sample Work 2

Write 30% as a decimal.

Solution

$30\% = 30$ ◄——— drop the percent sign and move the decimal two places to the left

$= 0.30$

To write decimal as a percent, multiply the number by 100 and then write the product with a percent sign. Or move the decimal two places to the right.

Sample Work 3

Write 0.42 as a percent.

Solution

$$0.42 = 0.42 \times 100 \quad \longleftarrow \quad \text{multiplying by 100}$$

$$= 4200 \quad \longleftarrow \quad \text{product}$$

$$= 42.00 \quad \longleftarrow \quad \text{move decimal two places to the left}$$

$$= 42\% \quad \longleftarrow \quad \text{write \% sign}$$

Sample Work 4

Write 0.03 as a percent.

Solution

$$0.03 = 0.03 \quad \longleftarrow \quad \text{move the decimal point two places to the right}$$

$$= 003 \quad \longleftarrow \quad \text{drop the decimal point}$$

$$= 3\% \quad \longleftarrow \quad \text{add \% sign}$$

Sample Work 5

Write 34 as a percent.

Solution

$$34 = 34 \times 100$$

$$= 3400$$

$$= 34 = 3400\%$$

Practice

Write as decimal.

1. 5%   2. 60%   3. 26%   4. 38%   5. 3%   6. 12%

7. 11%   8. 9%   9. 75%   10. 56%

Write as percent.

11. 0.02   12. 1.02   13. 2.5   14. .04   15. 0.22

16. 1.5   17. 130   18. 58   19. 0.16   20. 0.18

LESSON 7.3

WRITING DECIMAL AS A FRACTION

To write decimal as a fraction, identify (or look at) the decimal value in words. For example, .24 means twenty-four hundredths. Hundredths means the denominator is 100, so .24 is $\frac{24}{100}$.

Sample Work 1

Write 0.25 as a fraction.

Solution

$$0.25 = \frac{25}{100}$$

Sample Work 2

Write 0.001 as a fraction.

Solution

$$0.001 = \frac{1}{1000}$$

$$= \frac{1}{1000}$$

Practice

Write as a fraction.

1. .002   2. .01   3. .014   4. .52   5. 0.8   6. 0.10   7. .5

8. 0.64   9. .9   10. 0.03   11. .3   12. .04

LESSON 7.4

FINDING PERCENT OF A NUMBER

To find a certain percent of a number, first change the percent to a fraction or decimal and then multiply by the number.

Sample Work 1

What is 1% of 300?

Solution

1% of 300 = .01 x 300 ←——— change 1% to decimal

$\qquad$ = 3

1% of 300 = 3

We translate the word "of" to "multiplied by."

Sample Work 2

Find 2% of $400.

Solution

2% of $400 = $\frac{2}{100}$ x $400 ←——— change 2% to fraction

2% of $400 = 2 x $4

2% of $400 = $8

Sample Work 3

There are 300 students in the school. Fifteen percent of the students are on scholarship. How many students are on scholarship?

Solution

Total students: 300

On scholarship: 15%

$$300 \times .15 = 45 \longleftarrow \text{change 15\% to decimal}$$

Forty-five students are on scholarship.

Practice

Find the following.

1. 12% of 50 2. 50% of 12 3. 10% of 80 4. 25% of 120 5. 35% of 920 6. 15% of 30

7. 13% of 240 8. 30% of 900 9. 1% of 30   10. 1% of 350 11. 1% of 430 12. 2% of $85

13. 4% of $850 14. 16% of $100 15. 5% of $600

16. Find 80% of 90.

17. Find 7% of $700.

18. Find 32% of 560.

19. Six percent of the cost of a suit is $30. How much does the suit cost?

20. If 5% of the cost of books is $15, how much do the books cost?

MAKING PIE CHARTS AND BAR GRAPHS AND FINDING MEAN

Learning Points

In this unit, we shall

- define and construct pie charts and bar graphs; and
- find mean.

LESSON 8.1

MAKING PIE CHARTS

Pie charts may be used to tell the percent of people or things—such as girls, boys, women, and men living in certain city, town, or village. A pie chart is also called a circle graph. A pie chart is used to compare parts of a whole. In other words, the main use of a pie chart is to compare. It presents summary of a large data set in visual form. When we present items on a pie chart, we are able to easily determine which of the items is the most popular and the least popular. Items on a pie chart are shown by slices. For example, this pie chart has five slices.

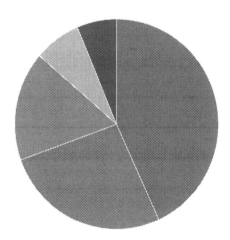

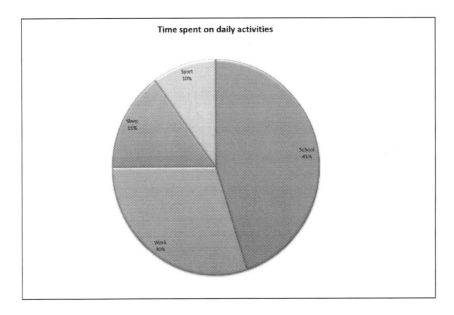

The pie chart shows the amount of time Dayugar spends on various activities during a day.

One may find it easy to read a pie chart. Look at the pie chart and figure out which slice of the pie is the biggest. Each bit of data is pictured on the pie chart as a pie slice.

You will observe that some data have larger slices than others do. From here, you can determine which data is more important than others are.

Sample Work 1

The pie chart below shows the percent of people living in Tarsonon Town with the population of 100 people.

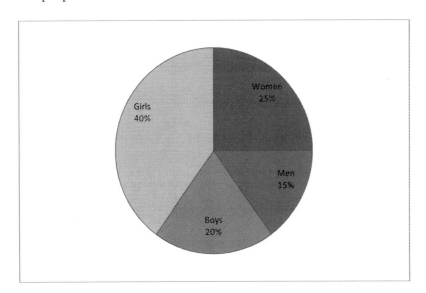

In Tarsonon Town:

1. How many people are women living in Tarsonon?

2. How many people are girls living in Tarsonon?

Solution 1: How many people are women?

25% women

So 25% of the 100 people $= 25\% \times 100$

$$= \frac{25}{100} \times 100$$

$$= \frac{25}{1} \times 1$$

$$= \frac{25 \times 1}{1}$$

$$= \frac{25}{1}$$

$$= 25$$

Twenty-five people are women.

Solution 2: How many people are girls?

40% girls

So 40% of the 100 people $= 40\% \times 100$

$$= \frac{40}{100} \times 100$$

$$= \frac{40}{1} \times 1$$

$$= 40$$

Forty people are girls.

Sample Work 2

The pie chart below shows the percentages of fifty third grade students who like different kinds of fruits.

a. How many students like grapes?

b. How many students like orange juice?

c. How many students like bananas?

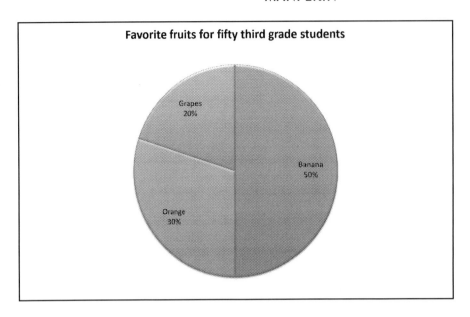

Solution

a. 20% x 50 = .20 x 50 = 10 students like grapes.

b. 30% x 50 = .30 x 50 = 15 students like orange juice.

c. 50% x 50 = .50 x 50 = 25 students like bananas.

Practice

Using the pie chart on page 128 about the people living in Tarsonon Town (Sample Work 1), answer questions 1 to 5.

1. How many people are boys living in Tarsonon?

2. How many people are men living in Tarsonon?

3. How many people are both women and girls living in Tarsonon?

4. How many people are both men and boys living in Tarsonon?

5. How many people are both women and men living in Tarsonon?

6. The pie chart below shows the percentages of the means of transportation two hundred students use to come to school every morning.

a. How many students come to school using bicycles every morning?

b. How many students come to school using cars every morning?

c. How many students come to school using buses every morning?

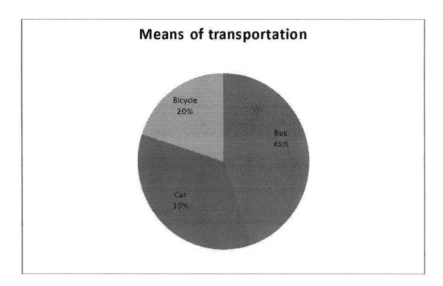

7. The pie chart below shows the percentages of 300 people living in four towns: Flumpa, Bunadin, Sokopa, and Beila.

a. How many people live in Flumpa?

b. How many people live in Bunadin?

c. How many people live in Beila?

d. How many people live in Beila and Sokopa?

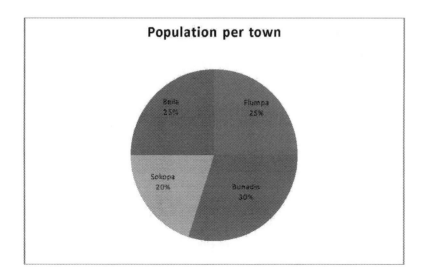

LESSON 8.2

MAKING BAR GRAPHS

A bar graph is used to compare between groups of different things. The bars show comparisons among the groups. The bars may be horizontal or vertical.

Bar graph with horizontal bars

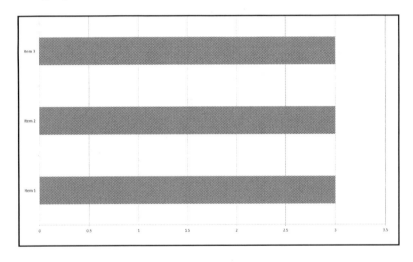

Bar graph with vertical bars

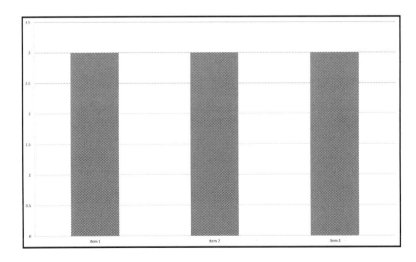

Sample Work 1

The numbers represent student attendance in the third-grade class at Duo School from Monday to Friday last week with the total number of students of 60. Draw a bar graph for the numbers: 10, 50, 60, 30, and 40.

Solution

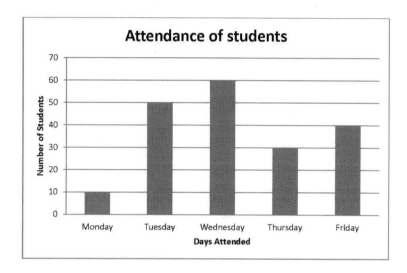

The length of these bars tells how regularly (or irregularly) students attended class last week on each school day.

Sample Work 2

The bar graph below shows the means of transportation that students use to come to school.

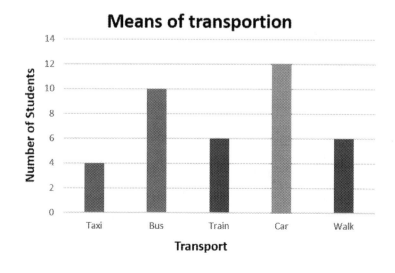

Use the bar chart to answer the following questions.

Solution

Questions	Answers
How many students come to school by means of car?	12 students
How many students come to school by means of taxi?	4 students
How many students come to school by means of bus?	10 students
How many students come to school by means of train?	6 students
How many students come to school by walking?	6 students

Practice

1. The bar graph below shows Weah's exam scores in various subjects during the fourth marking period. What score did he obtain in English? What score did he obtain in math? What score did he obtain in history? What score did he obtain in science? What score did he obtain in computing?

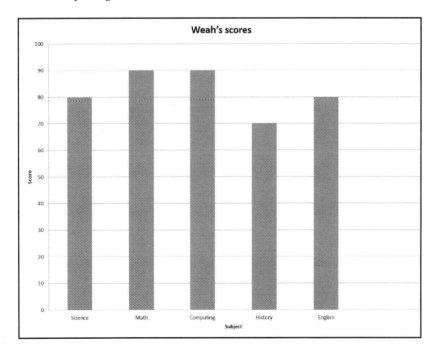

2. Dwalu records the amount of time he spends on five different activities within twenty-four hours and draws the following bar graph.

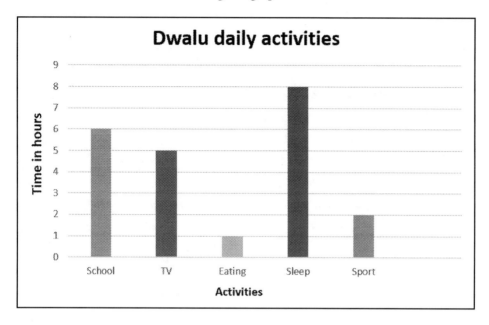

How many hours does he spend sleeping? How many hours does he spend in school? How many more hours does he spend in school than watching TV? How many more hours does he spend on sport than eating?

3. The following numbers are student attendance in the fourth-grade class at Vanjama Elementary School from Monday to Friday with the total number of students of 35: 25, 20, 30, 10, and 5. Draw a bar graph for the numbers and interpret the graph.

LESSON 8.3

FINDING MEAN OF A SET OF DATA

Mean is a single value or number that represents the whole group. To find the mean or average, add all the numbers and divide by the total number of data. Mean is another name for average of the numbers or set of data.

Sample Work 1

Find the mean (average) of the following numbers: 5, 6, 9, 8, and 7.

Solution

$$\text{Mean (average)} = \frac{5 + 6 + 9 + 8 + 7}{5} = \frac{35}{5} = 7$$

Sample Work 2

The second marking period test grades for four students in the second-grade class at Zorzor Elementary School are 80, 75, 65, and 73. Find the mean.

Solution

$$\text{Mean} = \frac{80 + 75 + 65 + 73}{4} = \frac{293}{4} = 73.25$$

Sample Work 3

The ages of six students in the fourth-grade class are 9, 10, 8, 12, 8, and 7. Find the mean.

Solution

$$\text{Mean} = \frac{9 + 10 + 8 + 12 + 8 + 7}{6} = \frac{54}{6} = 9$$

Practice

Find the mean for the set of numbers.

1. 5, 7, 3   2. 8, 1, 3, 2, 4   3. 1, 2, 2, 3   4. 8, 9, 7, 6   5. 80, 51, 95, 91

6. 76, 92, 98, 85   7. 58, 62, 90, 75

8. What is the mean of 33, 23, 26, 25, and 21?

9. What is the mean of 29, 32, 28, and 29?

10. Find the mean of the following set of numbers: 6, 4, 10, 11, 41, and 20.

11. Find the mean of the following set of numbers: 1, 18, 15, 10, and 3.

12. What is the mean of 542, 311, 412, and 657?

13. Find the mean of 14.2, 35, 56.1, 19.5, and 10.

14. Find the mean of 15.1, 13.2, 10.3, 20.4, and 15.

15. Find the average of Oretha's grades during the first marking period: 95, 88, 78, and 79.

16. Find the mean of this set of data: 211, 229, 341, and 451.

17. Find the mean of the following grades: 70, 85, 90, 66, and 78.

LESSON 8.4

PROBABILITIES

Probability is a chance of an event occurring.

Rolling a Die

A die has six sides. The number of possible events that occur when it is rolled is six. When we roll a die, we get six possible outcomes: 1, 2, 3, 4, 5, and 6. The probability of any one of these outcomes is $\frac{1}{6}$.

Sample Work 1

What are the chances of rolling a 3 on a die?

Solution

There is only one face with a 3 on a die. There are six possible outcomes when a die is rolled. So, the chances of rolling a 3 is $\frac{1}{6}$ This means that the probability of rolling a 3 on a die is $\frac{1}{6}$

This is the probability of an event happening divided by the total number of possible outcomes.

Flipping or Tossing a Coin

When we flip a coin, we get two possible outcomes:

- Head, which is represented by H

- Tail, which is represented by T

The probability of the coin landing H is $\frac{1}{2}$, while the probability of the coin landing T is $\frac{1}{2}$. This is because there is only one way of getting a head or a tail when a coin is tossed, and the total number of possible outcomes is only two.

Practice

Find the probability of the following:

1. Flipping a head on a coin

2. Flipping a tail on a coin

3. Rolling a 5 on a die

4. Rolling a 2 on a die

5. Rolling a 1 on a die

6. List the possible outcomes for tossing a coin.

7. List all the possible outcomes when a die is rolled.

ABOUT THE AUTHOR

S Pee N Vululleh, EdD, has several years of educational experience—teaching, developing educational material resources, and administering educational institutions. You may commonly call him Prof/ Dr. S Pee. He served as director at the Bureau of Teacher Education at the Ministry of Education for many years and provided professional training for school administrators. He also served as assistant superintendent for Monrovia Consolidated School System (MCSS) and made employment and staff benefits decisions.

S Pee participated in developing the Professional Standards for Teachers in Liberia and revision of the National School Curriculum. Prior to these services, he served as station superintendent and principal of Ganta United Methodist Mission, where he provided support to reestablish the vocational program at the school. He also taught at the University of Liberia Graduate Program in Education and United Methodist University for several years.

S Pee is an author of *Elementary Mathematics Grade 4* and a coauthor of math textbooks for ninth, eighth, and seventh grades for Liberian schools, entitled *Maths for Junior High for Liberia*. S Pee is a person with vision and is a consultant and innovator in the field of education. His main interests include research and developing human resources and causes of learning.

Dr. S Pee is a trainer and an author.

Printed in the United States
by Baker & Taylor Publisher Services